A *Perfect* WORLD

To the in-laws who I am most proud to call family
Polly & Bautam: May all your dreams come true!

Alan Finino

A *Perfect* WORLD

WORDS *and* PAINTINGS *from* OVER 50 *of* AMERICA'S MOST POWERFUL PEOPLE

Collected by Debra Trione

Andrews McMeel Publishing

Kansas City

*A*ttention: Schools and Businesses

Andrews McMeel books are available at quantity discounts with bulk purchase for educational, business, or sales promotional use. For information, please write to: Special Sales Department, Andrews McMeel Publishing, 4520 Main Street, Kansas City, Missouri 64111.

A PERFECT WORLD:
Words and Paintings from Over 50 of America's Most Powerful People

02 03 04 05 06 TWP 10 9 8 7 6 5 4 3 2 1

ISBN: 0-7407-2726-5

Library of Congress Control Number: 2002103639

Book design by Holly Camerlinck

For Paul, whose spirit inspires me daily

Contents

x

XI

Acknowledgments

My genuine admiration and thanks go to all the leaders who agreed to dream at least for the duration of our interview, and who had the courage to stretch their public personae enough to take on this unconventional assignment.

Many generous friends and family members offered their inspiration, encouragement, and advice, including Tim Madigan, Bonnie Abrams, Jonathan Rich, Bennett Barsk, Sarah Strum, Judd Rose, Mark Langer, Eva Peter, Sam Asher, Pearl Rubin, Philip Rubin, Lew Horowitz, Janet Trione, Walter Jaros, Edward Trione, Barbara Trione, David Trione, Cindy Mindell-Wong, Zena Collier, Colleen Buzzard, and Gary Tepfer.

Many thanks also to the children in my life who dream: Maya Jaros, Sarah Jaros, Alexis Hanley Trione, Adrienne Zand, Sonia Zand, Laura Rich, Miriam Asher, Leora Wong, Juliet Lande, Lee Lande, Eliana Lande, Judith Gibson-Okunieff, Kaila Gibson-Okunieff, Rachel Rose, and Jacob Rose.

This project was enriched enormously by the perspectives and professional counsel of Stephen Kosslyn, Fred Mast, Deborah Tannen, Steven Pinker, Gerald Zaltman, Robin Tolmach Lakoff, Eric Caine, Edwin Burrows, Dorian Bergen, Paul Nunes, Amy Huser, and my visionary editor, Jennifer Fox.

My deepest gratitude to Paul Okunieff, without whom this project would never have breathed life.

The idea of America is the idea of a perpetually perfectible world: "a more perfect union," states the Constitution; "a system approaching near to perfection," boasted Benjamin Franklin; "the world's best hope," according to Henry Cabot Lodge.

It is not an idea that Americans invented, of course, just one that we brought down to earth. Heaven may be reachable, but only after death. The Garden of Eden is ancient mythology; the Peaceable Kingdom, Never-Never Land, and Oz are literary constructs. And when Thomas More wrote *Utopia* in 1516, the name he chose for that imaginary ideal island was a word that in Greek meant "not a real place."

America made the perfect-world idea pragmatic and also built a national identity around it. While the citizens of most other countries share a common ethnicity, race, or religion, Americans delight in their distinctions. They do not look like one another, speak the same language, or pray to the same kind of God. But from sea to shining sea, they do share one rarefied presumption that

in any other country might sound pompous or absurd—the presumption that at least within those borders the best of what could be will closely resemble what is.

In a brilliant new book called *A Visionary Nation*, Zachary Karabell presents the entire sweep of American history as a series of national efforts to chase after one, and then another, perfect-world vision framed by a succession of idealistic leaders: the seventeenth-century Puritans, the Founding Fathers, the Great Triumvirate of the early nineteenth century, the robber barons, twentieth-century Progressives, and then a bevy of harbingers in our own time. "The quest for perfection has been a hallmark of American culture since a group of settlers embarked from the old world to create a City on a Hill," Karabell concludes.[1]

Yet it may be hard to see how such a quest animates the nation today. When I set out to learn how contemporary American leaders envisioned their ideal world, I ran into first one wall and then another. Early on I requested an interview on this subject with

Arthur O. Sulzberger, Jr., publisher of *The New York Times*, and he shot back an answer through the mail: "I'm afraid the idea of a perfect world is disturbing to me," he wrote. "For one, I'm not sure I'd have a place in a perfect world. Secondly, I'm not sure what the role of newspapers would be if everything was going swimmingly. 'Everyone Wins Lotto, Again'—I don't think so." Sulzberger's letter was unusually frank and funny, but the sentiment it expressed was surprisingly common: Perfect worlds are unsettling somehow, and besides . . . get real!

Maybe our current discomfort with perfect worlds grows naturally from the fact that we've shared our recent past with the most malevolent efforts ever recorded to manufacture perfect worlds at any cost: with Hitler's satanic Final Solution, with Stalin's collectivization through mass terror, and with the evident failures of Sino and Soviet social engineering. Visions of Utopia have so recently produced its dystopic obverse that conventional laissez-faire wisdom concurs: The best of all possible worlds can never be prescribed. If a more or less perfect world is possible at all, we can only imagine that it might emerge slowly over time in the messy push and pull of conflicting self-interests chasing private gains in incremental ways.

Yet the exercise of envisioning ideal worlds remains a good and even necessary labor, all the more so now that our civilization and science are starting to alter, and even control, many of the most fundamental systems that determine who and what we are (genetically, psychologically, chemically), what our environment is like, and which other living things share this planet with us in the decades and centuries ahead. By now, it is certainly not hard to imagine reconstituting the atmosphere, living hugely elongated lives, creating artificial life, or harnessing the otherworldly forces of quantum physics. And as human influence expands, the power of our leaders explodes. Fewer and fewer things happen without their blessing, or against their will. Which means above all that their ideas—their pictures—of a perfect world matter, and will matter more and more.

A problem arises, though, when powerful public leaders are judged to be smart and successful because they verbally twist statistics, skew logic, or leave topics just vague enough to satisfy the casual listener without triggering lawsuits or tripping any media alarms. Some questions ought to be—must be—asked of all national leaders, and they need to be answered in the most graphic and unequivocal way: questions about the big-picture priorities and ideals of those who have a privileged grasp on the coming course of events. The project documented here was a fresh attempt to ask some of those necessary questions and also to elicit some pure and spontaneous answers. If it's not too much trouble, sir, could you please just make it come straight from the shivering heart of your deep and secret soul?

I knew that to get that kind of candor, the assignment I gave these leaders had to be surprising enough that they couldn't form their answers easily into any kind of fudge.

All the interviews recorded in this book began in an unremarkable way. My questions were Rorschachesque—so broad and unfocused that they invited the heavy hitter sitting across the table to talk about almost anything positive that sprang to mind. "Name two or three things you hope will be true about the world in fifty or sixty years," I coaxed. "Tell me about the kind of environment in which you personally thrive."

But a few minutes into each interview, an excruciating awkwardness would always ensue, a pause during which the VIP would typically suspend his or her breath in broad-faced disbelief. That moment was always the one in which I pulled out a colorful selection of acrylic paints and oil pastels, and asked the leader to literally picture his or her perfect world.

"This is appalling to me," gasped Alan Simpson, sitting suddenly motionless and falling silent for a full minute or more, while a look of abomination played across his face. "This is not an area of my brain that I normally call into play," complained James Fallows, holding on to the last breath he had taken just before I brought out the paints, his eyes dashing lightninglike around the room. "I can't think of anything more difficult to do," Patricia Ireland protested, sucking in air, holding it, then dropping her head with a barely audible moan.

Much to their credit, Simpson, Fallows, Ireland, and many other notables did eventually take to the task. Every time one of them did, a flush of excitement would pass across my neck and boil up the surface of my face. Something alchemical was going on. A whole new category of document was being forged in real time and right before my eyes. Never before had people of this caliber been willing to describe their "visions" in real visual terms.

Before I talk about what vital new things these interviews and images add to the public record (more than to document, for instance, that this country is currently being run by some really bad artists), I want to first mention that collecting this material was often a laugh-out-loud hoot. I remember, for instance, that Daniel Goldin, then chief administrator of NASA, was so energized by the painting assignment that he kept leaping up from his chair during our session. This would have been fine, except that my tiny tape recorder was attached by a wire to a microphone clipped to his collar. Every time Goldin blasted skyward, the recorder would sail off the table into the great beyond so that more than once I had to jump up to snatch it back. This may have fully terrified me then, but it seems quite funny to me now.

As a figure of speech, "vision" is something that every leader has to have. Who would follow a person without it, someone drifting aimlessly at the whim of circumstance or chance? But there are also substantive and serious reasons to ask all people with power and influence to paint (rather than sing, dance, or recite poetry about) their notion of an ideal world.

The first involves a simple truism: Any visual image that persists in our mind, any image remembered or rehearsed, exerts a dynamic but stealthlike force that tries to carry the reality described by that image into being. The unique force that a compelling mental image can exert is so powerful and mysterious that cognitive scientist Stephen Kosslyn, who has studied mental images in his Harvard laboratory for twenty years, calls them "ghosts in the mind's machine," independent operators that drive our actions and determine our direction according to the inexorable logic of their own design.

The self-realizing energy that lurks in mental images has been noted for centuries and across cultures. It is the muscle that activates prayers and the inspiration behind the ancient Latin axiom *Fortis imaginatio generat causum* (A strong imagination begets the event itself).

Archaeologists even believe that the self-projecting potency of mental images may have been the very force that spurred our Paleolithic, cave-dwelling ancestors to make the first pictures ever carved or painted onto stones. Those earliest images ever do not after all depict the world as the cave dwellers saw it, but the world as they wanted it to be—the Paleolithic version of a perfect world. In one set of such paintings (dated 15,000 to 10,000 B.C.E. and still visible in Spain), deerlike ruminants succumb dramatically beneath brilliantly targeted arrows and spears. In a roughly contemporaneous set (in France), grazing herds amass across the walls and ceilings of caves in such fantastically improbable numbers. It seems that our early ancestors worked hard to harness the self-realizing power of imagery, just as they may also have struggled to tame any other dynamic force of nature, fire or wind.

It's easy to dismiss these cave paintings as products of a primitive preoccupation with the occult, forgetting that even today, and without any hocus-pocus, the cave painters' magic still moves us.

Picturing, or "visualizing," a desirable outcome is still the surest way to achieve that end, and every motivational trainer knows it. Goal visualization exercises are now standard practice in rehabilitation therapy, business motivational courses, weight-control regimens, career development strategies, and Olympic sports. Every commercial advertiser knows that a compelling visual image can nestle down into a semipermanent niche in the customer's mind, a site from which it then transmits the steady, barely detectable drone: "This is the way things are; this is the way things should be." (Of course, the image in any advertisement will always be one that requires product X, sold now at some location near you.) The prehistoric magic pulses on.

If mental images are powerful motivators, then the mental images held by powerful people should be matters of public concern. I had expected the paintings I collected from these modern-day chiefs to reveal something new about the potent but intangible phantoms that might be compelling the very people who in turn are controlling this nation of ours. But when I showed a few of these paintings to a friend of mine who is also a curator at a major American art museum, he balked. "These are not mental images," he said, "they're paintings! If these people had been using cameras instead of paint, you'd be looking at some very different pictures."

But that is precisely the point. Medium matters, and this is a new one, in which (along with their words) the exceptional leaders featured in this book agreed to describe their visions for a better world.

Marshall McLuhan was the one who, back in the 1960s, popularized the notion that no medium is neutral. Every medium—speech, film, radio—operates as a distinct vehicle for conveying its own unique category of understanding, using its own vocabulary, with its own endemic set of weaknesses and strengths. It must be better, richer, then for our leaders to express themselves in more than one format, especially now that our verbal language is so often crafted to confuse.

Of course these paintings are not the one-and-only true reflections of the inner contents of these leaders' minds. Countless real mental pictures must constantly arise from the deep organic stew of new impressions and understandings. The pictures shown here were made not only in a very particular medium but also on very specific days, and under the unique social and political circumstances of a certain season and hour. I interviewed John J. Phelan, Jr., the recent chairman and CEO of the New York Stock Exchange, in his Manhattan apartment just nine days after terrorists destroyed the World Trade Center towers a few blocks away. Would his comments and his painting have been different on some other day? Probably yes. But if these paintings represent at least some approximation of some of the previously unknowable, never-before-seen portraits of

perfection held in the minds of these national leaders, then they are certainly precious and rare.

If every medium is uniquely suited to conveying certain kinds of truths, the paint medium used here might best convey truths about conviction, veracity, authenticity, and credibility—the very qualities of communication that are so often hidden beneath the spoken or written language of people with power. And this might be especially true of these particular paintings, which were all created on the fly, without much warning and with no professional counsel at all.

Since all paintings are made over time by a human hand, one way to read them is certainly similar to the way anyone can experience and find meaning in body language. That is, every painting can be understood empathically to imply a formula for the flow of our energy. It can embody a pattern of enthusiasm, pleasure, or rage, the imprint of a tender or plodding hand that we register instantaneously as having proceeded and then paused before moving swiftly or cautiously on. This is important because visually perceived body language has long been considered the single component of communication that is most difficult to fake.

It was once commonly thought that only those few individuals who possessed an uncommonly keen intuition could discern the so-called hidden messages contained in a slightly arched eyebrow or a sudden blush. But in fact so many people can so accurately and instantaneously "read" the meaning of visually perceived body language that our laws and customs assume this ability outright. (Jurors, for instance, are routinely required to be physically present at a trial, in part so that they may better assess the veracity of each party's claim by watching the comportment, and looking into the eyes, of accused and accuser alike.)

Brain physiology probably has everything to do with the fact that we consider visual signals the best barometers of sincerity and conviction. As recent research has shown, most visual information is processed in the nonverbal right hemisphere of the brain, the same brain area that makes sense out of the animal-like gestures of fidgets, cuddles, cries, grimaces, smirks, blushes, and body stance. Signals like these are universally understood to be less responsive than speech to conscious will or volition and more reflective of deeper, truer, more candid states of being.

> *What a man is begins to betray itself when his talent decreases— when he stops showing what he can do.*
> —Friedrich Nietzsche

One day I arrived on time to interview a high-level federal official, only to be kept waiting in the lobby outside his office for a full twenty minutes, while (I later learned) a media adviser tutored the VIP on how he should answer the questions they expected me to ask. When the much-anticipated one-on-one finally began, the adviser abruptly decided to join us, first planting his elbows forward on the table, then leaning like a dog at a dinner dish into our conversation. Just until I pulled out the paints. I am certain that that was the precise moment when the adviser began slowly collapsing backward into his chair, letting out a soft but audible moan, and no doubt checking this interview off as a total and humiliating loss. It was the purest form of satisfaction I could have hoped for that day.

When I started this project, I wanted somehow to assure that these paintings would be as perfectly sincere and spontaneous as possible. So I deliberately chose not to interview anyone known to be a painter. All the painters featured here were awkward and ill at ease with the medium, inexperienced at choosing colors, and ponderous about pushing paint around on a flat surface with a brush. And just to further compound any deficit of virtuosity that they may have naturally possessed, I sprang this difficult assignment on each of them with little warning, knowing that the pressure of their schedules would dictate that they spend no more than twenty minutes painting. Dan Goldin could have been speaking for many when he confided that "the last time I did this was maybe kindergarten or first grade."

On the other hand, not a single one of these painters was illiterate in the language of visual communication in the same way that one can be illiterate in, say, Portuguese. Visual literacy is universally assumed these days because visual communication is so ubiquitous. Who does not routinely make sense of illustrations, glossy mailers, computer screens, TV advertising, or family snapshots? How many of us have trouble deciphering graphs, disentangling maps, or interpreting picture books, picture postcards, or color slides?

The paintings in this book are not arbitrary, mindless, or interchangeable. All the VIP painters thought hard and took the assignment seriously. I never broke down any doors or twisted any arms. All the leaders agreed willingly and even graciously to paint. And, despite their inexperience, most of them finally did find a way to convey an idea or picture a circumstance that had particular resonance with them. The fact that they failed to manipulate the paint with artful grace only makes these paintings better, more candid records of their ideals. "All bad poetry springs from genuine feeling," said Oscar Wilde,[2] and the same could be said of bad painting, except maybe even more so.

I confess that I began this project not only hoping to uncover the pure and candid truth but also with a blithe preconception of what that truth would be. In 1994 and '95, I had served as a task force liaison on the President's Council on Sustainable Development, an improbably diverse selection of real-world leaders: Fortune 500 CEOs, high-level federal officials, and representatives of several large nonprofit advocacy organizations, whose institutional agendas were often (at least apparently) at odds. Yet our council's mission was to devise and then clearly articulate a set of win-win policy recommendations to promote (simultaneously, no less) economic, environmental, and social well-being. It all seemed pie-in-the-sky impossible at first. But in the first several months, during which we tried to reach consensus on broad, big-picture goals, there turned out to be a remarkable degree of harmony throughout (even if the devil really was lurking in the details).

That experience seeded this book. I proceeded with the same underlying aim of uncovering the broad and big-picture ideals of real leaders. I also deliberately chose to interview a wide variety of powerful people, fully believing that most of their big-picture hopes and dreams would turn out to be pretty much the same. And I imagined that this book would be a warmhearted demonstration of just how much we all have in common, in spite of our contentious habits and confrontational ways.

That is why I felt so confounded at first by the baffling range of this material. Some of the leaders I interviewed for this book wanted to talk about the best of all possible futures; others remembered a simpler, more Arcadian past. Some described and drew from their personal experience; others pictured more global or abstract themes. For some, a single image sprang immediately to mind. Sometimes that picture was of a particular place and time, a distinct moment that embodied perfection in a jewel-like way. I had imagined that they would broaden their perspectives and see the forest for the trees, but instead many collapsed the rarefied notion of an ideal world into a supersaturated essence, and then cast about for a graphic way to describe that essence whole. A few evasively restated the question. Still others pictured a landscape of favorite things, an eclectically assembled perfect-world pastiche. Many of the advocates conceived of an ideal world remarkably like the very world we live in now, absent just one or two big problems—a world with more A, less B. Others scribbled the trajectory of desirable changes they wanted to see occur. And a very few had so much trouble evoking any image at all that a disconnect developed between what they could easily articulate in words and what they were able to put down in paint.

I needed some help making sense of this weedy cacophony of paintings and perfect-world descriptions, so midway through this project I decided to show the material to several language and image experts, including Harvard Business School professor Gerald Zaltman, an authority on imagery in advertising.[3] Where I had seen a seething anarchy of attitudes and approaches, Zaltman recognized concurrence. He noted immediately, for instance, that both General H. Norman Schwarzkopf and Carnegie Endowment for International Peace president Jessica Mathews had described their perfect worlds as places of peace, and that both had pictured human figures standing amid similarly tranquil mountain scenes. "That causes us to think that the goals of these people may not be so different, and I find that quite compelling," Zaltman remarked to me over the phone. "If you had asked these two people to picture the means rather than the ends, you might have gotten Schwarzkopf to paint a strong military and Mathews to draw a conference table. But the painting assignment you gave them caused them to cut through the polemics of 'How do you get there?' and go on to 'Where is it you want to go?' The good news is that they do have similar goals. So to me the pictures are more important than the words."

Zaltman was right, of course, to notice a certain amount of consensus in these works. Several common and recurring themes do run through the verbal descriptions, while a somewhat different set of leitmotifs weave through the pictures. No one will be greatly surprised to discover that values such as peace, racial harmony, population stabilization, and a narrowing of the gap between rich and poor were common in statements from a wide range of leaders. (If I had interviewed more leaders after September 11, 2001, ending terrorism might have been high on everybody's list.) At this telling, though, education seemed to be the number-one priority for nearly everyone: liberals, conservatives, doctors, lawyers, generals, businesspeople, and politicians alike.

Nature showed up less frequently in the statements and more often in the paintings, a point that didn't pass unnoticed by urban historian Edwin Burrows.[4] "As a historian of one of the world's great cities, I couldn't help notice how little we see here of human effort and achievement," Burrows said with some indignation over the phone after I showed this material to him. "What's most surprising is that the painters are people who spend their time working in large communities—armies or organizations or political movements. I would bet most of them live in cities. It's human association after all that gives context and meaning to our lives, and yet I didn't see much of that in the pictures. What they painted was a pretty characteristically American way of looking at things, the Daniel Boone mentality that if you can see the smoke from the other guy's chimney, you're too close."

I also showed this perfect-world material early on to cognitive psychologist Steven Pinker,[5] who, like Burrows, was quick to pick up on the preponderance of nature in the paintings, even if he gave it quite a different spin. "What's most interesting is how many of your respondents chose scenes from nature," Pinker remarked. "I think a deep part of human nature feels most at peace in a particular natural environment—one with greenery, with open areas punctuated by trees, with water, and animals. That's the habitat that our species evolved in, and thrived in, and that extends itself into our brain. In the biblical story we came from the Garden of Eden, and in the visions of a number of your respondents there's an eco-paradise that may be the kind of environment in which our species feels happiest, and that people use to symbolize an ideal world."

"On the other hand," Burrows had said in a matter-of-fact tone at the end of our conversation, "if I were the one doing this assignment, I'd probably end up painting much the same thing." Nature is easy to paint, he said. "It's much more challenging to represent a complex human-built environment."

This is an important insight. It might explain, for instance, why some themes that are common in the spoken statements never appear in the paintings, and vice versa. Pinker was now warming to the subject. "The two things I study as an experimental psychologist are language and imagery," he said, "so this speaks to the heart of what I do." Pinker noted, for instance, that it may be easy to talk about, but very hard to paint, the absence of something—a world

without A or B. I had asked each leader to describe the world as he or she wanted it to be, but many had used that question as a springboard from which to launch into a dramatic description of the world's most urgent problem as they viewed it that day. Their perfect world was simply a world without hunger, terrorism, homophobia, et cetera. "This highlights one of the key problems in pictorial representation," said Pinker. "Concepts like the absence of something are impossible to draw unambiguously. A room with no giraffe in it is identical to a room with no elephant in it, or no cockroaches in it. So in order to indicate which concept you have in mind, you've got to use language.

"And another reason we need words," he went on, "is that what people really value is often not purely visual but really also reflects their interpretation. If I open my eyes and see New York, or I open my eyes and see a picture of a fake New York on the wallpaper in a Las Vegas hotel, they may look identical. But one of them is actually thrilling and valuable, and the other one is tacky. The difference is in my knowledge of what those shapes and colors mean, rather than in the actual image. I thought Kiplinger's painting was terrific, by the way. He did a lovely job illustrating what is a very abstract philosophy. But unless you have the words, you have no idea that those arrows are supposed to stand for free, self-organized economic systems. I think if you were to hide the verbal text that accompanies any of these paintings, very few people would have any idea what they stood for."

Fair enough. I hadn't planned to hide the text and look at the paintings alone. But that turned out to be exactly what the Harvard psychologists Steven Kosslyn[6] and Fred Mast decided to do when I showed this material to them. Using twelve of these paintings but none of the verbal descriptions, Kosslyn and Mast devised a psychology experiment in which they asked several subjects to rank how similar each painting was to each other painting, first in terms of appearance and then in terms of underlying meaning or message. Their study assumed, in other words, that—contrary to what Pinker thought—people could derive meaning from pictures that are not accompanied by words.

Once Kosslyn and Mast had collected the data, they used a mathematical technique to draw up two charts, on which all twelve paintings were placed relative to one another, first in terms of appearance and then in terms of meaning. (Paintings rated as similar were placed close together; those rated as dissimilar were placed far apart.) Some fascinating patterns emerged. Who would have thought, for instance, that in terms of both visual similarity and conceptual similarity, Gary Bauer's painting of a perfect world would rank so close to James Carville's? Or that Congresswoman Nancy Pelosi and Patricia Ireland (two left-wing, feminist women) would rank so far apart on both charts? The more the reader knows about the public alliances, agreements, rivalries, or points of contention between or among these

public figures, the more significant and sometimes shocking will these paintings and their statements seem.

The Kosslyn and Mast experiment cut right to the chase. Instead of dwelling on what any one statement or painting might tell us about its creator, they asked a more important set of questions. What do all the entries together tell us about the relationships between and among these varied individuals and their agendas? Are the paintings done by bitter public adversaries as different from each other as one might expect? What about paintings done by allies? What are the dominant and recurring themes, and is there any unexpected convergence of ideals? What are the axes along which these people seem to differ or agree? Do these paintings clarify or uncover anything new about the goals and aspirations of these influential somebodys that their words alone cannot convey? What differences are there between what these people articulate and what they paint? Or between what they expressed during these interviews and what they assert publicly in real life?

I have been careful not to answer any of these questions myself, in part because that is what I want the reader and viewer to do. New and surprising clues lie here within these pages. Crack open the book and see.

Footnotes:

1. Zachary Karabell, *A Visionary Nation: Four Centuries of American Dreams and What Lies Ahead* (New York: HarperCollins, 2001), p. 9.

2. Oscar Wilde, "The Critic as Artist," in *Collins Complete Works of Oscar Wilde*, centenary ed. (Glasgow: HarperCollins, 1999), 1148.

3. Gerald Zaltman is the Joseph C. Wilson Professor of Business Administration at Harvard Business School and the inventor of the Zaltman Metaphor Elicitation Technique (ZMET), used to discover imagery that may be influencing behavior below the conscious level.

4. Edwin Burrows is the Broeklundian Professor of History at Brooklyn College, CUNY, and winner of the 1999 Pulitzer Prize in history for *Gotham: A History of New York City to 1898*.

5. Steven Pinker is the Peter de Florez Professor in the Department of Brain and Cognitive Sciences at Massachusetts Institute of Technology and author of *How the Mind Works* (1997) and *The Language Instinct* (1994).

6. Stephen Kosslyn is the John Lindsley Professor of Psychology at Harvard University and author of *Ghosts in the Mind's Machine* (1983) and *Image and Brain* (1994).

A Perfect WORLD

Marcia ANGELL

Editor in Chief, The New England Journal of Medicine *(1999–2000), Executive Editor (1988–99)*

Marcia Angell, M.D., became the first female editor in chief of *The New England Journal of Medicine* in 1999, after having served as executive editor since 1988. She retired from the journal in June 2000 to become senior lecturer at Harvard Medical School. She is a prominent authority on medical ethics and the author of *Science on Trial: The Clash of Medical Evidence and the Law in the Breast Implant Case.* In 1997 *Time* magazine named her among the Twenty-five Most Influential Americans.

What I very much hope for in the broader world is that we reach some better understanding of the relative place of the individual and the community—where individualism is legitimate and where a more cooperative community effort is legitimate. I think we often get that wrong. What we see often is a kind of rampant individualism in the economic sphere, which is tantamount to vital things like food, housing, medical care, and the use of natural resources. We have a frontier or entrepreneurial spirit about that. You get to do whatever you want. You get to make as much money as you want, or starve to death if you want. And a few people corner the goodies of the world at the expense of much larger numbers of people. We've made health care into a commodity. You get what you can pay for, and you get far more than you need, and far more than is good for you, if you can pay for it. If you can't pay for it, you don't get anything. The same thing is true of food and housing. We see wagons drawn up around the affluent and educated, and the devil take the rest.

I think that's wrong. It's not compassionate, and it doesn't work. We truly are seeing problems now that I think could destroy civilization as we know it: the depletion of natural resources and overpopulation, which in some sense has to do with capitalism, since having a lot of children is the only way under this system that poor people can take care of their health-care and old-age needs.

At the same time we're seeing a kind of groupthink about cultural and personal things. The political correctness movement annoys me because it asks everybody to think alike; nobody can hurt

3

When you say "an ideal world," I think first of an orchestra, outdoors like Tanglewood, but not as commercial, and without all the New Yorkers with their candelabras. But this assignment is limited by my capacity to draw. I can't draw an orchestra. I've never done this before, so I'll just have to draw what I can.

4

anybody else's feelings, everybody has to like the same movies, and there's a homogenization of culture.

People think that television is bringing democracy to the world. It's really bringing capitalism, not democracy. Everything is for sale; everything is a contest; everything is combat. Sports is combat; politics is combat. Who's going to win? Who's going to lose? And that's a very primitive way to look at things. So, this is where we should have individuality, and yet this is where we act like we're all members of a coral reef.

What I want to see is that we have a very strong sense of community in terms of taking care of one another's essential needs and sharing the goodies. I would gladly pay far more income tax if it went toward this kind of sharing, because I know I've been very lucky. No special virtue, I've been lucky: I've been loved; I've had people care about me; I've had the chance to develop my talents. And there are people who are unlucky. But even if you look at it in the capitalistic way—that people deserve what they get—nobody deserves to starve or die of an illness just because they didn't plan better or weren't good at the stock market. It's a punishment way beyond the crime of being lazy, or whatever other personal failings capitalists assign to poor people. What I want to see is for people to feel much more of a sense of obligation to each other.

The other thing that disturbs me is the dumbing down of an already privileged people, largely through television. Both of my grandfathers went to school only through the third grade, but they could read and write, and were highly competent people with skills a lot of college graduates don't have now. They had to read, write, learn geography, learn history, learn arithmetic, and they got whacked if they didn't learn it. Now we would consider this pretty primitive, but it was better than nothing, and what you get now is a lot of nothing. What we used to learn in high school we leave off to college, and now everybody's got to go to graduate school because college is just a place to drink beer and get together. So, the rigorous work of learning is increasingly postponed and childhood extends longer and longer.

My perfect environment on a personal level has three components. I like to be in a community that has a rich cultural and intellectual life, where there's a lot of music in particular. Then at the same time I very much like open spaces and emptiness, so at least every year I go out to the Southwest or Northwest: Montana or Utah.

And the third thing is work. Work is extremely important, and I have to believe that my work matters, that it can have an effect. I'm not so simpleminded as to think that I could change the world for the better, because I don't see the world moving that way. I see the world as being one step forward, two steps back, and three forward. It's more like a body of stagnant water that laps up and back, and up and back. I don't see any overall progress or regress. But I still feel it's important to work toward making it better, even if in the long run it doesn't mean a hill of beans. To have been here for a lifetime and not to have tried is just wrong. *November 26, 1997*

Norman AUGUSTINE

President, Chairman, and CEO, Lockheed Martin Corporation (1995–97)

Norman Augustine served as president of Lockheed Martin Corporation, the dominant defense contractor in the United States, beginning with the founding of that company in 1995. The following year he ascended to the rank of CEO and later chairman. In 1997 he joined the faculty of the School of Engineering and Applied Sciences at Princeton University. He previously served as chairman of the American Red Cross, and as president of the Boy Scouts of America. Augustine was listed as one of Fifty Great Americans by the Library of Congress and *Who's Who in America*.

Let me just say as a caveat that I have spent most of my life worrying about the next quarter's earnings, so to stand back and imagine what an ideal world would be like is refreshing, but not something I've devoted a lot of thought to.

For the larger world I would clearly hope that people could learn to get along better, that we wouldn't have the kind of inhumanity toward others that we see now on a national basis in wars, and on a personal basis where one person hits another person over the head to take his tennis shoes. I would hope that diseases could be cured, not necessarily to extend people's lives, because we probably live long enough already, but so that the lives we do live can be more satisfying.

I'm particularly concerned about the growing distance between the well-off and the not-well-off, the haves and have-nots. I also worry about the race between the drive to understand one another better (with our greater mobility and communications technologies) and on the other hand the deep-rooted misunderstandings and hatreds that still exist. I worry that the increased mobility and anonymity that go along with today's society make it a lot easier for terrorism to operate on a big scale.

I travel a lot, and I personally have friends all around the world. It's rare that I don't like the people I meet once I get to know them. It's very rare, even if they're very different from me. But by the same token I think we could be in for some very rough surprises in the near term, with terrorism.

I can neither paint nor draw very well, so making this painting will be a big challenge. It's going to be tough. Actually, this is kind of fun. This painting is a combination of happy places—oceans, mountains, and valleys—all mixed together. I think the secret is knowing when to quit. Okay! I give up! I quit! Look, you can almost tell it's a mountain.

7

Among the projects I've enjoyed the most has been building Lockheed Martin as a corporation. I wanted to help build something big, and it happened to be a corporation.

I also worked many years ago on a missile range where we flew missiles, and I loved that because you could see your results instantly—either they blew up or they worked. It was a very real world, where real things happened, and they were important things, we thought. We were judged by Mother Nature, rather than by a group of lawyers, or whatever. I found that particularly rewarding. I've also found the things I've done for the Red Cross and the Boy Scouts to be very rewarding, because you feel like you're helping people. I've been involved with the Boy Scouts for over fifty years, most recently as president, and am heading toward nine years as chairman of the American Red Cross.

If I had a lot of extra money to give to one cause, I'd use it to help young people get an education. I might spend it on university scholarships to help good students—motivated, dedicated, who try hard but who don't have the money to go to college. I myself went to Princeton for six years and never paid a penny. I was the first in my family to go to college, and the second ever to attend high school. I got a scholarship, based on need. I don't even know who helped me pay, but were it not for them, I never could have done it. And in my life, college made a huge difference.

It's amazing how a few moderate decisions here and there have made all the difference. I don't think I have many real regrets. I can't think of too much I would have done differently. I've made some bad business decisions from time to time, but if I were to run out of runway tomorrow, I'd still have to say it was a great life. And so be it. *July 23, 1997*

Gary BAUER

Candidate for U.S. President (2000); President, American Values (since 2000); President, Family Research Council (1988–99); Domestic Policy Adviser, Reagan administration

Gary Bauer was a candidate for U.S. president in the Republican primaries of 2000, running on a strong pro-life, pro-family, pro-growth agenda. After the elections, he became president of American Values, a family-values advocacy organization, and chairman of the Campaign for Working Families, one of the largest political action committees in the country. Before that he served as president of the Family Research Council, a public-policy organization, for ten years. During the Reagan administration, Bauer was assistant to the president for policy development and director of the Office of Policy Development in the White House.

When I think of what I hope for in the world, I must admit that I tend to think in terms of America because we have such incredible influence around the world. We export our culture for better or worse. First of all, I would hope for a country in which there is respect for life again. Now when I say that, the first issue that comes to mind is abortion, and that certainly has been a central issue for me over the years. I would like to see a world in which women never find themselves in pregnancies in which they have been abandoned by the men in their lives and have to face this terrible option. But, more broadly, I see a continual erosion of the notion of the sanctity of human life.

In the United States partial-birth abortions take place in many cases in the last trimester—in the seventh, eighth, or ninth month. These are babies who, if just delivered, would live, and there would be people who would be willing to take them. There was an article in *The New York Times Magazine* by an ethicist who suggested that we really ought to lower the penalty for infanticide because a newborn baby, according to him, really isn't fully human, in the sense of having a range of experiences. Now the fact that *The New York Times* would put this in their magazine is, I think, a sign of the real erosion of the idea that life is a sacred thing that ought to be taken only under the most extreme circumstances.

My ideal world is a world in which our children are taught that life is sacred, no matter how many times they see people being blown away on television or in the movie theater. Our Constitution

This painting is probably the most difficult thing I can imagine doing. I'm a very uncreative person. I was standing in some other line when those skills were given out. Well, I guess I could just try to paint a house because I do think the home is the center of life.

grants a tremendous latitude in the name of free speech, and Hollywood is going to be able to produce what it wants under the law. But I would love to see a future president call Hollywood producers to the Oval Office and publicly rap them on the knuckles for their pollution of our culture. By using the bully pulpit of the White House, a president could really shame these folks who are making a great deal of money serving us gore and violence.

In most of my speeches I try to encourage audiences to recapture the idea of America as a shining city upon a hill. This country was supposed to be a unique place built around a set of values. But that concept of us being a shining city might be in jeopardy. I think the jury's still out over whether or not we'll be able to pull back with some core values again, or whether we will define America as merely a place offering the liberty to do anything we want, whenever we want it, which, I think, would be a disaster.

One of the biggest things that's happened politically in the last twenty years has been the reluctant but growing involvement of conservative, traditionally oriented people in the public square. If that continues over the next twenty years, they could transform the culture and our national politics.

On the other side, pulling against that, is the fact that we've got a science in America today that's running way beyond our ethical and moral calculations. For instance, all the genetic engineering things that are beginning to break on the scene, the whole cloning issue, which twenty-five years ago looked like fanciful science fiction. People are beginning to sense that the world is spinning out of their control, that men in white coats are making decisions, and whatever decisions they make, the rest of us will have to accommodate ourselves to. Of course, there's some hope in medical breakthroughs, but there's also a lot of danger. The biggest danger being that people will be seen as nothing more than protoplasm to be manipulated and experimented on.

There's already talk, for example, of creating a subspecies. They've grown frogs and tadpoles without heads to see if the other organs develop correctly, which apparently they do. And some scientists are talking about doing the same with humans, only obviously they wouldn't be humans because they'd have no brains. That's the worst of eugenics—creating a subhuman species to cannibalize for your own purposes. We defeated Hitler on the battlefield, but his bizarre theories, unfortunately, still have some power. Only it's with highly educated elites who don't see the moral implications of some of these things.

If I had a lot of resources, I would use them either to try to rebuild the family unit, which is disintegrating not only in America but in all the Western democracies, or to try to promote the idea of fidelity and lifelong commitments and keeping promises. It's easier to get out of a marriage in America today than it is to get out of an aluminum siding contract.

There's a phrase we use often in evangelical circles that wives are to be submissive to their husbands. But biblical submission is a much broader concept than we think of in the secular arena today. In fact, the verse goes on to say that men are to love their wives and children and to sacrifice for them even to the extent that Christ sacrificed for the Church, being willing to die for them.

At the risk of sounding overly dramatic, one of my favorite places is the Vietnam Memorial. To me, it seems like a uniquely American place. It strikes me that in this city that revolves around movers and shakers—the Speaker of the House, the Chief Justice of the Supreme Court—those individuals are just passing through; they have power for a season, and then they're gone. The notion of sacrificing yourself for someone else, or for a greater cause, is something that transcends politics. Though politicians try to use the rhetoric of sacrifice, unfortunately American politics usually plays itself out as the exact opposite. It's all about getting power and keeping power. But the memorial represents something much more permanent, that speaks of the notion of sacrifice, and duty, and honor. So that has become a place that I often visit on my own.

I recall that when I was growing up my father was an alcoholic and we were a working poor family, so there were some real difficult times. I remember wondering what a good family life would be like, and I had a hard time envisioning being married and doing the things I'd need to do to have a successful home. But when I fell in love with Carol and we had children, I had no idea it would be as rewarding as it has turned out to be. Now when I think back, being there to see the birth of my child, working through some of the things we had to work through in the marriage, or seeing our kids really excel at something and begin to feel their own way—those clearly have been for me the most rewarding things in my life.

December 10, 1997

Harold BLOOM

Author; Sterling Professor of Humanities, Yale University

Harold Bloom is the Sterling Professor of Humanities at Yale University, where he has taught since 1955. Widely considered to be one of the greatest living literary critics, he is the author of numerous books, including *The Book of J* (1990), *The Western Canon* (1994), *Shakespeare: The Invention of the Human* (1998), and *Stories and Poems for Extremely Intelligent Children of All Ages.* (2002).

One wants what any tired, old, worn-out democratic socialist like myself would want: a more equitable society. But I know we're not going to get it. We are such a strange country. I can't really hope for much for a country that is as wackily religious as ours.

Based on the latest Gallup polls, this is a country where something like 90 percent of Americans say they talk to God, and he talks back to them. Short of only Ireland, there is nothing like such a percentage anywhere in the world. That same 90 percent say God loves them on a personal and individual basis. That makes me think about one of my heroes, Baruch Spinoza, who said that we should learn to love God without ever expecting God will love us in return, which is most un-American, to say the least.

I think the United States is a kind of post-Christian country which continues to think of itself as Christian, but that its Christianity has almost nothing to do with historical, institutional, dogmatic, European Christianity. There's a kind of indigenous American religion that started about two hundred years ago, with a big frontier revival in Kentucky and Tennessee, that has gone on ever since—a very peculiar fervor.

Fortunately, we are also a country that worships the Constitution. Look, every hour on the hour I turn on the television to hear the latest dreadful thing that's going on in Kosovo. This is the madness of religion. Orthodox Christians killing Moslems because they're Moslems. Religiosity is a terrible thing. I would like to see a more secular United States, but I don't think it's going to happen.

I also haven't got much hope for the future of American politics, precisely because it is all mixed up with American religion. I suppose if one could have a more secular society, then it might eventually be a more equitable society. Actually, I am so disaffected about what goes on culturally in the United States that I don't know how much difference that makes to me anymore.

What you might call High Culture seems to me to have been destroyed in the United States over the last thirty years by multiculturalism. Education has become debased. My own profession has sold the past to all this multiculturalist nonsense. The teaching of literature has become a nightmare. Universities aren't interested in literature anymore.

So, you know, obviously I would like to see all this multicultural garbage come to an end. But I think there is not a chance of that. I think, instead, literary study is coming to an end. I have seen only intellectual decline in the English-speaking world for the last thirty years. We have an entire generation, two generations by now, who really believe that class, gender, race, ethnic group, sexual orientation, determine everything. If you're a human female, they expect you to be a so-called feminist literary critic, which as far as I'm concerned is like the Holy Roman Empire—it's not holy, it's not Roman, and it's not an empire. The notion that a piece of writing is of particular value because it was written by a woman rather

than a man, I find infuriating. Of course, it has taken over the universities. Things have now reached a point where someone like myself, who believes that some books are intrinsically better intellectually and aesthetically than others, and who tries to insist upon canonical standards, is regarded as a rather extreme reactionary.

I do have an answer, it turns out. What I would like to see is universities where the faculties answer the real needs of undergraduates in the old traditional way, rather than by trying to impose an ideology upon them. I want the idea of disinterested inquiry to return, but I don't think it's going to happen. We've fallen into an age of ideology.

Well, look how little use I'm being to you. You're interested in people's utopian visions, but I don't think I have any, dear. I do care about teaching, though. The sense of being able to provoke students into becoming themselves rather than a digest of others, that's rewarding.

I think the prevalence, and the oddity, of American religion has something to do with the lack of values in our education. I am mystified how we became a nation where people just don't care to read anymore. Here is a nation that doesn't seem to think, doesn't seem to read, doesn't know how to argue, can't see clearly. The problem, I think, is a visually based popular culture, which does serious harm to the young.

The idea I grew up with and that I thought I would achieve in a lifetime of teaching literature was that what finally matters is the

My drawing will be, I suppose, a young lady reading a book. (Not a very handsome young lady, since I can't draw very well.) Based on my experience as a teacher at Yale these last forty-six consecutive years, the good solitary readers I know are more usually young ladies than young men, but not always. So, rather crudely, it's a solitary reader.

15

solitary woman or man who finds herself or himself by going off and reading and thinking. On that basis, the reader really gets to know the best of what has been thought and said, and individuates himself or herself, which now sounds banal. *June 5, 1999*

Julian BOND

Chairman, National Association for the
Advancement of Colored People (since 1998)

Julian Bond became chairman of the National Association for the Advancement of Colored People (NAACP), the nation's oldest civil rights organization, in 1998. He is a legendary civil rights pioneer, active since the early 1960s in aggressively advocating for racial and economic justice. He is also a distinguished history professor at American University and the University of Virginia, and a frequent radio and TV commentator. Bond served ten terms during the 1960s and '70s in the Georgia state congress, where he sponsored or cosponsored more than sixty bills that ultimately became law.

I'm most comfortable as part of a group of people working for social change. That's the kind of environment I've spent most of my adult life in. And the one I felt most engaged in was the Student Nonviolent Coordinating Committee, where I spent five years, between 1960 and '65, working for social change nearly twenty-four hours a day, seven days a week. There was a lot of energy and we were all young, with few other responsibilities. I was married and had children, but almost no one else was. No mortgages, no car payments, none of the impediments of modern society. We were paid very poorly. Most people lived and ate communally in freedom houses. I felt more involved then than I ever have since, which is not to say that I haven't enjoyed what I've done since then, I have. But I felt more in touch with my co-workers and the larger world than I ever have since.

We also had a certainty that we were right. I had an absolute certainty that we were absolutely right, and of course time has proved us to be right. Not to say that we didn't make mistakes, because we did, some of them very egregious. But we knew we were right, and we had the conviction of the righteous, which is an enormous armor that enables you to just plow straight ahead.

Part of the optimism I feel today comes from the work I've done in the civil rights movement and seeing results. When my students today tell me that race relations are awful, that they've never been this bad, I'm old enough to remember when they were *much* worse. And I'm old enough to remember how they got better: by ordinary people doing extraordinary things that created a move-

17

*W*ell, this is a novel idea. I should have paid more attention in art class.

That's me! It's a self-portrait; I'm sitting in a chair reading a book, maybe a true crime book, or a history book—twentieth-century American history, not European. It could be a British detective novel, or maybe a newspaper. It would be in my home. The chair is green, and there're books on the facing wall, and then windows on these two walls. So I'm looking out into a yard, which is not very large, but it is very green. It's a relaxed, peaceful setting. I really wish this painting could have been better, but you either have it or you don't. I'm attracted to primitive art, naive art, or folk art. I have a lot of it in my house. I think it influenced my piece.

ment that made presidents and congresses and state legislatures use their power to create progress or to ratify progress that had already been made.

So even though there had been two Supreme Court judgments mandating the integration of interstate travel, interstate travel was still not integrated. It took the freedom riots of 1961, with people getting beaten and put in jail, to finally make the federal government enforce those two Supreme Court decisions. Nothing happened until people felt summoned to move and confront segregation, expose the lengths to which the resistant white South would go to maintain the system, the brutality they'd engage in, the connivance of politicians with that brutality. All of that so horrified the country that they insisted the government should act, and the government did act. It was done.

So I'm optimistic based on my experience. And I do think that history shows a gradual social improvement over time. In race relations I've seen that improvement over my lifetime. Race relations in this country have always been on an up-and-down, and sometimes even a forward-and-back, course, but the end result has been improvement. The forward push is too strong to be anything but temporarily turned back. At least that's my hope.

The NAACP has been, for all of its existence, a bourgeois organization. That was true when it was founded, and it's true today. One of the ironies of its success has been to create a wider gap between the classes in black America. So no longer does the doctor live next door to the ditchdigger, and you no longer have this cohesive black community that we once thought existed all over America. That is not altogether a bad thing. We tend to romanticize that community, when in fact it had its own internal class divisions. The doctor's daughter and the ditchdigger's son didn't play together, even though they lived next door. But class divisions within the black community have become in some respects more pronounced.

However, I don't think that has seriously affected the effectiveness of the NAACP. We see our aim as the elimination of discrimination, through litigation, legislation, and lobbying. And it really doesn't matter what our makeup is, as long as we're made up of people who, regardless of their station in life, are committed to the task. My ideal would be for every black American to belong to this organization. But that has never been true.

Of course, in this country in general I'd like to see the enormous income gap close between the people who work on the factory floor and the people who own the factory. It's just horrendous that in America it's getting wider, wider here than in Britain or Germany or Finland or France. It's scandalous, and it's a prescription for enormous social disorder. Of course, I'd also like to see race relations improve radically. I'd like there to be a strengthened body of law to deal with discrimination, but I'd also like to see a consciousness in the country that didn't require a prompting by law. I'd like people to say, "I'm going to do this because it's the right thing to do."

If I had a large amount of cash to give to one cause to improve the world, I'd probably give the money to some form of lower education: first, second, third grade. It seems to me that we're failing children down there, more than at the college level. Young people from the meanest circumstances can do well, given the right opportunity. (Not every single one of them; some have personal problems too great to be overcome.) But many can whiz right through like champions given the right opportunity and some encouragement, and I don't think we give it to them.

One of my favorite places in the world today is my home—the house I live in with my wife. It's physically attractive and comforting, a refuge. Almost everything I want is right there. I'm a book person; I have all my books there. I'm a popular music and jazz person; I have a big collection of music. I seek . . . Everything is there.

March 31, 1997

David BRODER

Pulitzer Prize–winning Political Correspondent,
The Washington Post

David Broder is a Pulitzer Prize winner (1972) and a pioneer in the full-time coverage of the process and issues that shape national politics, political campaigns, and presidents. Aptly described as "the dean of American political writers," his twice-weekly column is syndicated by the Washington Post Writers Group to more than three hundred newspapers worldwide. When a younger reporter asked him how to cut through political poppycock, Broder famously advised him to "trust your eyes."

For the larger world, I would love it if every child who came into the world was a wanted child, with parents ready and eager to help that child achieve his or her potential. When you get to be an old fart like me, you've seen some remarkable things. Certainly I've seen great changes in this country with regards to the relationships between, and the status of, men and women. There's much more gender equality now, not just in the workplace but, I think, in the home as well, which is a very welcome development.

There's been some progress in race relations, too. I mean, this newsroom is much more integrated now than it was when I first came to work here, and that's a great benefit. As a white male who presumably was the loser in affirmative action, my professional and personal life have benefited enormously from this company's affirmative action program. I have colleagues and friends now whom I literally would not have had. It's difficult, in my experience, to develop close friendships across racial lines without the glue of workplace experience. I have a few close friendships with African-Americans whom I've gotten to know through work, and that's been a great enrichment in my life.

I also feel blessed to have worked at this paper at the time that I did. I've been here for thirty years, and was here during Watergate. It probably wasn't the best time to be a reporter in Washington, but the combination of Katharine Graham, Don Graham, Ben Bradlee, and a lot of other people made *The Washington Post* just about as perfect a place to be a reporter as you could ever have hoped for. They gave us all the resources we could ever want, with very few hang-ups, and tremendous—no, total—commitment to making the paper just as good as it could possibly be. That's a rare thing.

I don't really expect we ever will have total peace in the world, but I do wish we had a regime that could deal with conflicts before they took an enormous number of lives. And I also hope for a world in which more people could share the material and political benefits that we take for granted in this country.

I'm not worried about power slipping away from the media. In fact, in some respects we've gained power, but not to the advantage of the country. I was just listening to Senator Bob Kerrey of Nebraska talk about how important it is for people to get reengaged in civic life. He said, "I'm for this bill, but the bill isn't going to change things. What's really going to change things is if people decide that it really is worth their while to engage again in civic life, which millions of people have turned away from now."

One of the basic arguments I've made repeatedly is that there's been a power shift from political parties to interest groups. Both of them have been and remain important parts of our system of self-government. But interest groups, because they have a narrower agenda and a more self-interested constituency, tend to protect the benefits that their constituency already has. Political parties historically have been great instruments for leaders to build public support for significant changes. Now, more and more people feel they're best represented not by political parties but by interest groups, and those interest groups, almost by definition, are protectors of the status quo. *June 16, 1997*

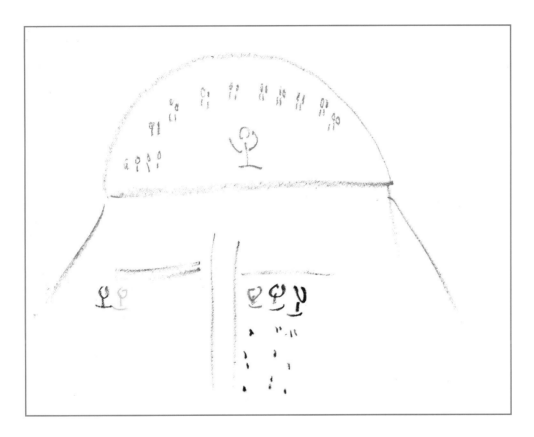

I have a pretty clear image in my mind of a perfect world, but I'm not sure I can draw it. I told you I was bad. You can see that music is one of the great joys of my life. What this painting shows is a concert hall: a conductor, a symphony, and an audience made up of all kinds of kids. Music gets me thinking and feeling good things. So my sense is that, if all young people had that opportunity, it would be a pretty good world. Symphony music, that is. You can't go too wrong anywhere from Mozart to Copland. They'll do very nicely, thank you.

My wife does all kinds of handwork: drawings, soft sculpture, paint, watercolors, needlework. She is going to be so envious when I get a drawing published. Will it be the end of a beautiful marriage? She won't believe me when I tell her!

23

Deb CALLAHAN

President, League of Conservation Voters (since 1996)

24

Deb Callahan became president of the League of Conservation Voters, one of the nation's most effective environmental organizations, in 1996. Before that she served as campaign manager for the successful reelection of Congressman Howard Wolpe and as director of the grassroots environmental program of the W. Alton Jones Foundation.

The first thing that springs to mind when I think about constructing an ideal world is that it's important for people to understand their own power. Individuals can have an impact on the world. We live in a democracy founded on the belief that an individual's opinion makes a difference. And I hope that humanity continues to evolve that way. There's a tendency for people to feel powerless. Yet as individuals we create the world we live in whether we sit around all day or get up and act. Everybody has to visualize where they want the world to go.

I also hope desperately that our governments and our people find a way to live sustainably on the earth, and that there will soon be highly evolved, sustainable, and diverse societies around the world.

I've been exposed personally to some extraordinarily bad places, towns that have had smelters and lead mining going on for a hundred years, so that an entire community for three generations has been lead poisoned. I saw a place in Colorado where there was unregulated methane gas pumping and the gas sometimes came out of fissures in the rocks. I was in a woman's home when she turned on her kitchen faucet and lit a match on the "water" that was coming out.

But I've also seen some spectacularly scenic sites of biodiversity, places that are quietly and extraordinarily beautiful. As a scuba diver, I'm really drawn to marine ecosystems where there are beautiful corals, and fish and marine mammals. You see so much biodiversity down there. You know when you go hiking in the forest you have to really pay attention, because things hide under leaves

This is a picture of everything at once: green mountains, pine trees, a little path, and a little bridge over a river with a lot of white water. What started out as a black bear sort of changed into a black elk. And the sun is coming up and the mountains in the background with the reds in the sky, and a storm brewing. It's light and energy, a peaceful scene where there's a place for everything. The world exists like this already, just as I've painted it. It's not a question of whether we're going to get this, because we've got it. The question is whether we're going to see it, and appreciate it, and keep a lot of the natural world from disappearing from the planet.

25

and in bushes. But fish frankly don't have many places to hide, so they're right there in front of you, and it's a very intense visual experience.

Probably one of the most powerful and amazing places I've ever been in my life was a research station in the middle of the Brazilian rain forest, where I went with Tom Lovejoy. About twenty of us climbed up onto this old rickety radio signal tower that went way above the canopy of the rain forest in the very early morning. So we were standing on this tower when the sun came up and the tropical birds woke up. And there was a fellow with us, who's now dead, but he was at the time considered the world's best bird-watcher. (This was just a matter of months before he died.) So about twenty of us were up at the top of this rusty tower that hadn't been inspected in years, and this guy who was the excellent birder would yell, "Look over here, there's twelve Hyacinthe macaws flying that way!" And twenty people would run that way, and the tower would go *errrrrch!* And one other guy and I would run the other way, just to be a counterweight. It was extraordinary being above the rain forest and watching these flocks of purple and red and yellow plumage, and seeing the clouds in the sky, and all the rain forest laid out below.

I believe in the basic good nature of people, and I believe that individuals really want to do the right thing. Having information is certainly not the whole answer but, absent information, people cannot act correctly. Making sure that people are informed and empowered is one of the best ways to ensure that our world is really a place we all want to live. So I would really like to enable people to exercise personal power in democracies. It's hard to assess macrostructures in society, but you have to do it, or they'll just run off with their own little agendas, and suddenly the citizens are not in control at all. Here in America, it's easy to find out how our elected officials vote on environmental issues, but in England and Canada, not to mention the Middle East, or Central or South America, citizens don't have any information at all about what the decision makers are doing.   *February 18, 1997*

26

Daniel CARP

Daniel Carp became chairman and CEO of Eastman Kodak Company in 2001 after having served in the company's top executive management for several years. He is also on the board of directors of Texas Instruments and a member of the U.S.-China Business Council and the Business Roundtable. He is an executive member of the World Business Council for Sustainable Development.

I thrive when I'm with a lot of people, where the creativity is generated by the energy of a group. And the group is not all people like me, white, fifty-one-year-old males who understand marketing. It has to be a diverse group; otherwise you can all agree before you go into the room. I get most of my satisfaction working with teams on tough problems. They have to be tough. If they're trivial, I get very bored very fast. Having the group come forward with sets of solutions to be evaluated and carried forward . . . I would rather be with a group of customers or Kodak people working on a problem than anything else in business.

It's a strange job being president and CEO. While it looks broad, it's actually very narrow. Most of my information comes through my business. That's just the way it is. I spend very little time looking at successes, because I'm constantly trying to shore up the problems. So if I'm not careful, I slip into the attitude that the whole world is a problem.

In a personal sense, I get total satisfaction when I'm with my family. So the combination of a job that requires 190 percent of my time and being able to have the personal satisfaction from my family is about all I can do.

In my perfect world, we would have reestablished or resupported the family infrastructure. And by that I mean we would be taking responsibility for one another, and have pride in the connectivity we have in our families.

You've got the least creative guy! I can't believe you're doing this to me. In the fourth grade when the class did a Christmas poster, they let me go work on math, so that I wouldn't damage it. That's a true story!

I do have a vision of what I want this to look like, but I don't know if I can communicate it with paint. This is basic, but you can see what I'm doing. We need to finally break through on diversity. Accepting people on a global basis for who they are, whether they're yellow, black, white, or red. A big part of my career has been outside the United States, so I have a fundamental belief in this. We could rebuild the family structure and we could learn diversity in its broadest sense. That would be my perfect world.

Your value system has to come from somewhere, and I believe grandparents and parents have a big impact on that. I also believe that young people today, who in my view are far ahead of my generation in terms of accepting differences among people, have something to teach us. But the breakdown of the family unit, whether because of distance or divorce, or the stress of having two people working, means we have lost a link of learning, and that's a big waste.

Actually, maybe this relates back to my love of groups. I mean, you need diversity not just in terms of race or religion but diversity in terms of age and experience. Technology would actually enable and help us in that. Things like computers, e-mails, digital pictures, can help the family unit stay connected if we value that, and work hard at it as a global society.

If you're in a society where people don't move away, it's easy. But if you come from the United States, and now even in some Asian societies, the kids are moving away from the family structure for opportunities. It's a very big loss.   *September 26, 1999*

James CARVILLE

Political Campaign Consultant and Adviser; Cohost, Crossfire, *CNN (since 2002)*

30

James Carville is a political consultant best known for having steered the successful gubernatorial campaigns of Robert Casey in Pennsylvania, Wallace Wilkinson in Kentucky, and Zell Miller in Georgia. He guided Bill Clinton to the U.S. presidency in 1992, from the famously fearsome campaign headquarters dubbed the War Room. Carville also consulted on the political campaigns of English prime minister Tony Blair, Brazilian president Fernando Henrique Cardoso, and the former Israeli prime minister Ehud Barak. In 2002 Carville became cohost of *Crossfire* on CNN.

Probably the environment I'm most comfortable in is my immediate family, my family from Louisiana, as most people would be. But professionally I thrive with intense projects of short duration. I like campaigns because there's a day certain when the project is over. I mean, when you win, it's sort of an intense burst. The longer the project, the less well I do. If I were a kid today, I'm sure I'd be diagnosed with attention deficit disorder. Back then they didn't know what it was, but I would have been when I was a kid.

My first hope for the larger world would be that more children are raised with a father in the house—in a traditional, two-parent family if you will. Look, I didn't get married until I was forty-nine years old, and I had my first kid when I was fifty—late in life. So having kids hasn't changed my political persona or my beliefs, but what I worry about has changed drastically. I worry more about my own children. What's going to happen to them? Where are they going to go to school? What's their life going to be like? How much time do I spend with them?

A second hope I have for the world is that we would see some greater progress made toward raising wages and standard of living for middle- and low-income wage earners. And the same thing for people in the Third World. I mean, obviously you also want the larger things like peace, vaccines, and disease eradication.

If I had a lot of extra money to give away, I guess I'd give it to some type of educational thing,

I've got to tell you, I'm not a very visual person. You want me to draw an image of what a perfect world is? Okay, my perfect world would have a daddy, a momma, two children, a book, a paycheck, and a future. That would be my kind of a perfect world. A better future or something like that.

31

having to do with developing skills. You know a lot of older people need to be retrained. Somebody could be thirty to thirty-five years old, caught up in a changed economy, and need a new set of skills. I'm a huge, huge believer in adult training. I think community colleges are the wave of the future. We don't have a problem at the top, with people who go to college and get advanced degrees. I would concentrate more on the middle and the bottom.

I'm not against it, but, like most people, I worry about the consequences of technology. I think what happens a lot of times is that we need fewer people doing more difficult things. So my first concern is, how can we do the best for the bottom half? In really, really poor countries, like, say, Honduras, as factories or textile mills become more and more efficient, they need fewer and fewer people to work in them. So I worry that there's less and less a place in the world for undereducated people. There never was a great place for them, but it's becoming less and less. The thing I like best about America is that the chance for upward mobility is better here than anywhere else.

You know, I think the smartest thing that's ever been said in the history of the entire world is "Change is certain; progress is not." (Put second the one about graveyards being full of indispensable men.) But that would be the first. I guess I'm a person with faith in the idea that we're learning better how to manage change, as a society.

You know the ethnic composition of America changed drastically around the turn of the last century, and it's going to change radically in the first twenty years of the twenty-first century. I'm not saying that's a bad thing, I'm just saying it's a thing. It's going to have an impact. I probably worry most about the impact it's going to have on the people already here—that they're going to recoil. Racism, bigotry, xenophobia, I'm not optimistic that any of those things are going away. But things have changed.

Look at Bosnia. If ethnic slaughters like that would have happened thirty years ago, you would have had two reporters coming out writing up a story in *The New York Times,* and it wouldn't have had the same impact, if you will. I'm not a historian, but we had a huge reaction in this country to a guy standing in front of a tank in Tiananmen Square. Fifty years ago, the tank could have blown up a quarter of a million people, and no one would have either known or cared. So I don't think the passions, the bigotry, the kind of hatred, are gone. I just think we've made it harder for bigotry to manifest itself. So in that sense things are changing for the better.

I've done a lot of work in politics around the world, and people are more accountable now. No one dares anymore to think about staying in power after their term is up. And so, while the media very often do not get it right, by the same token, instant communications makes it harder to get away with the darker side.

July 22, 1998

Robert CHASE

Robert Chase was elected president of the 2.6-million-member National Education Association (the nation's largest professional employee organization and teachers' union) in 1996. He developed the NEA into the nation's premier champion of quality public schools, frequently advocating for public education on national media, including CNN's *Crossfire*, NBC's *Today* show, PBS's *NewsHour with Jim Lehrer*, and ABC's *Nightline*.

There are too many flash points in the world right now because of religious and ethnic intolerance. If you look at the Middle East or Northern Ireland or Bosnia, people have long-term, firmly held beliefs that are maybe not based upon, but certainly are built upon, hatred for other people because of who or what they are. What I want to see is the elimination of those kinds of sectarian, ethnic, religious, racial conflicts.

My ideal environment is one where people are challenged to think and expected to take risks, an environment that celebrates diversity of opinion, that encourages debates. I'm serious about this. I mean, I think that often we just allow ourselves to change from one box to another. I want an environment where there are no boxes. If you have only like people—all white men, all black men, all white women, all Hindus, all Catholics, whatever—then after a while it's not challenging.

Diversity of people is what makes for diversity of ideas. My folks, who lived through the Depression, would talk with me about the Depression, and I studied about it as a history teacher. But I can't really understand the Depression because I didn't live through it, so there's no way. And for me to try to understand another person of another ethnicity or race or religion without interacting with them . . . I'll never be able to do that. And I particularly can't understand them if I just listen to people who are like me. I have to experience it through the eyes of the people who have had that experience.

34

I'm thinking of a print of a painting by Picasso that my daughters gave me. It shows a circle of children holding hands, and each one is a different color. You can see, obviously, the green is the earth, a whole, bright sun, but with a nice gentle rain connected with it. There should be some kind of rainbow here, too. Then kids of all different hues together, smiling, happy. Five different ethnicities. I'm not an artist, so what can I do? It's just this gentle sun and gentle rain and a rainbow.

My perfect world is a world where people have an opportunity to be whole. I have an idea in my head about what it means to be a whole person, but I don't know exactly how to describe it. You need confidence in yourself. Part of it is having the willingness and the inner strength to take risks, to know that it's okay to make mistakes. If you're not willing to make a mistake, you won't try to do things differently.

You have to be able to dream; you have to be able to take risks and make mistakes. But you also have to have some kind of reality base. It's important to create a capacity for people to fight the battles, take them on, develop the skills, the knowledge, the abilities. And, obviously, education is the thing that does that.

I remember Senator George Mitchell talking about a high school English teacher of his. He said he never really read until one day when he went to this English teacher and saw a book of hers that he liked. The teacher said she'd loan it to him if he'd read it. So he did read it, and then he came back and she gave him another, and then another, and then another. She opened up a whole new world for him. That's the kind of thing that makes you whole, that makes you a person: the ability to read, to dream, to develop the intuitive understanding you need to know where to go and what to do.

I just think that if we were to put our trust in our children and give them what they need to succeed, over time the world would be a much better place. But instead we too often bring them up with the same hatreds and prejudices that we harbor, and we sometimes create young people who are incredibly self-centered. I'm not naive enough to hope for a world where there's no competition. That's part of the human spirit, and that's good if it's done right. In the long term the best way to change things is to deal well with our children when they're young. If we educate our young people, if we inculcate nurturing values in them, it will break down a lot of problems.

October 22, 1997

Linda CHAVEZ

President, Center for Equal Opportunity
(since 1995)

Linda Chavez is president of the Center for Equal Opportunity, a nonprofit public-policy research organization. President George W. Bush nominated Chavez for U.S. Secretary of Labor in 2001. She subsequently withdrew her name from consideration. In 2000 she was honored by the Library of Congress as a Living Legend for her contribution to the cultural legacy of America. During the Reagan administration, Chavez served as White House director of public liaison (1985) and staff director of the U.S. Commission on Civil Rights (1983–85). She writes a weekly syndicated newspaper column and is the author of _Out of the Barrio: Toward a New Politics of Hispanic Assimilation_ (1991).

I would like to see virtually everyone in the world living under a system in which they are able to freely elect their leaders. Large parts of the world, and the biggest country, China, do not have democratic forms of government.

On the whole I'm a chauvinist when its comes to Western civilization. I think the idea of the individual endowed by the Creator with certain inalienable rights is a tremendous advance in human history. And it's a conception that changes everything. You know you can't just mistreat people. You can't decide that just because a person is poor or from a tribe that's not your own, you can treat them badly. This is the basis on which democracy is built, and I think the world will be a much better place if the Western idea of the individual proceeds. But it also needs to be tempered, because I think in some ways the United States has taken a very radical view of the individual. The individual is godlike.

I'm not a Libertarian. I think you have to have some sense of community in addition to individual rights, and I think it's a very fine balancing act.

I was also very distressed on a number of levels by the last election. I'm distressed that in the United States only about half of the eligible people actually voted. I would have to be very, very sick to miss voting on Election Day. It also distresses me that a lot of people are very ill informed and just vote according to which person they like more. That bodes badly for the future of democracy. I

I'm not an artist, but I was thinking of a lake in Colorado where I like to walk called Indian Peaks. It's in a wilderness area just at the edge of Rocky Mountain National Park, and my husband and I often go hiking there. So I guess that's the two of us. My ideal world. This is a really neat project.

mean, our founders conceptualized a civic body that was educated and focused enough to know what the issues are. So there's lots of work to be done, even here.

I would also like to see every child born into a two-parent household, where it was wanted and loved. We've seen enormous changes in the last fifty years in the structure of the family. We now have a third of all American children (two-thirds of all black children and half of all Hispanic children) born out of wedlock. That bodes very badly for the future, because we know that that situation severely limits the life opportunities of those children. We've had a dramatic shift in our conception of marriage, which has been very bad for women and children, and I think also bad for men. It's been bad all around.

We've actually had a decline in marriage, not just an increase in divorce. Some of this has had to do with government policies, but it's also had to do with changes in popular culture and attitudes toward sex. We need to reinvigorate the concept of marriage and the idea that you get married *before* you have babies. When you pick a marriage partner, that's the most serious decision you'll ever make. You should go into it with the expectation that it will be a lifelong commitment.

I really thrive with my family around me, so I guess that has been the most fulfilling part of my life. I'm fortunate to have three happy, well-adjusted, successful sons living close by. Two of them work for me. Having kids who like to come home for Sunday dinner—we really are a very close family. I talk to my kids every day, and I'm involved in their lives.

One of my very favorite places is my front porch, where I look out at the hills of Virginia, part of the Blue Ridge chain. I live on nine acres, and I have very open expanses that were obviously at one time farmland. So they're very lovely. I've also got a couple of horses and three dogs and a parrot. So sitting on my rickety-looking front porch in a rocking chair and looking out at the vista is one of my favorite things to do.   *August 23, 2001*

Linda CHAVEZ-THOMPSON

Linda Chavez-Thompson was elected executive vice president of the AFL-CIO (American Federation of Labor and Congress of Industrial Organizations) in 1995, becoming the first person of color to hold one of the federation's three highest offices. She is also the highest-ranking woman in the labor movement. She served previously as vice president of the AFL-CIO, beginning in 1993, and as national vice president of the AFL-CIO's Labor Council for Latin American Advancement from 1986 to 1996.

I want an America that recognizes the talents of all people, even those who don't have a college degree. I do not. But I had skills; I had a talent, and someone recognized it. There are a lot of people who are not "college material." Give them an opportunity. I got mine. Open opportunities for people and let them become what they can.

I love to make changes that bring people a better work or social environment. What can we do to give people a higher standard of living? I've worked very hard; I've lived on the road for the last two years to make this happen, to make this world better for working people. And I've done it all for very selfish reasons, extremely selfish: so that my grandchildren and many thousands and millions of other grandchildren will have a better life. That's it.

We talk a lot about race and poverty in America, and a lot of the problem is that people are not given the proper training, the skills that will launch them into the world. Our educational system isn't geared to those who don't go to college. Some school districts don't allot money for vocational training. Or the job fairs they have do not include, say, carpenters and plumbers and semiskilled workers, or say, "Look, if college is not for you, you can still get a job that pays twenty dollars an hour with benefits. Even without college you can do good for yourself and your family." Sometimes the schools don't allow books about labor unions. We see kids in college who have no idea what a labor union is. People who don't want to go to college are made to think they're not as

39

I'm drawing a world of people of all colors around the country, around the world, celebrating who they are, and joining hands to help each other. It happened in Boston, where a group of Latino women worked at a curtain factory and the company refused to recognize them, or even give them rest-room breaks. They got the church leaders, the community leaders, the union leaders, the whole community, to march and picket against the company, which eventually did recognize the union because it became so embarrassing to them. We have to bring that kind of community effort back into play around America.

good as other people. They deserve a level of respect. It's okay not to go to college, if that's what they choose.

I'm a people person. I love to be in contact with, and communicate with, people, whether it's my family or through the labor movement. As a young child I hung out with my two older sisters, so I grew up fast emotionally and mentally. I was never without an opinion, and my opinions were always better than anybody else's. I thought I knew everything. I was a very egotistical child. So eventually my brothers and sisters began to believe it, too. It was always more about perception than anything else, and that's something I've used in my labor career, too. I just take my very loud personality in and let people believe that I'm in charge. If they ask, "Where do you get this power?" I just tell them I have it, and they believe me.

What I want for the world is good training, good jobs with good wages and benefits for everybody. Also, respect and dignity for who we are culturally and ethnically. Respect the race you come from, respect the culture you come from, and don't divide us by the black and white paradigm. We're all Americans, no matter what our culture, no matter what our race.

As a young woman, I felt there was supposed to be something shameful about being Mexican-American. It was the perception that Mexican-Americans are not as smart and don't have skills and talents that should be valued. I've had to learn pride in where I come from.

I think we need better education. We have so few opportunities out there for minorities to read about their history, about their culture, or about where they came from. Most of our history books paint a bad picture of the Latino community. Yet, here we are, descendants of Aztec kings and queens.

I think the dialogue on race that President Clinton initiated opened the minds of many people who felt very secure that they were not part of the racial divide in America. "I'm a liberal, so I'm okay." Oftentimes those people had their own biases, perhaps unknown to them. And they were reluctant to talk about race. "I'm okay on that subject, next subject." They didn't want to recognize it.

Of course it's true that some groups use the charge of racism as a crutch. If you blame the other guy and think all your problems are caused by someone else, you're not doing yourself a favor. We have to do something about changing that image ourselves. We should get in knee deep and begin to change the direction of the swirling waters ourselves.

We have recently been emphasizing diversity within the unions, bringing in not just more people of color but also women into leadership positions within the union. It seems to be working.

January 20, 1998

Robert COONROD

President and CEO, Corporation for Public Broadcasting (since 1997)

Robert Coonrod was appointed president and CEO of the Corporation for Public Broadcasting (CPB) in 1997, after serving as executive vice president and chief operating officer beginning in 1992. (CPB is a private, non-profit entity created by Congress to develop noncommercial telecommunications services for all Americans.) Before joining CPB, Coonrod was deputy managing director of the Voice of America, the global radio and television network.

42

Of course the most rewarding experience in my life was when I became a parent. That's obvious. There's nothing quite as rewarding as being part of the march of the generations in a very specific and very human way, so that it is not abstract but a very concrete experience.

Beyond that, I think the most rewarding thing is just the feeling that we grow in wisdom and understanding. Sometimes you appreciate that, and just sort of hit your head and say, "Wow!" I want to live my life more consciously and more effectively today than I did ten years ago, and believing that I will is a source of tremendous satisfaction. The progress of life is really progress toward becoming more conscious.

It's hard to articulate, but I was married for a long time, and then I got divorced. Now I'm not married, but I do have a long-term relationship with the same person, and my involvement in those two relationships—how I relate to the other person—is profoundly different. I'm more tolerant, more demanding, and much more conscious of who I am, what motivates me, how I respond to things, and what it means to be a person. I don't think I could have done this sooner in my life. When I was twenty-one, this wasn't available to me, even though I had the kind of consciousness even back then that was inevitably going to go here.

One thing I hope for in the world is for people to find a way to express their spirituality without interfering with the way other people do it, that it could be done in a noncompetitive way.

Human beings have always looked for ways to express their sense of the transcendent, the spiritual. But that's impeded in all kinds of ways, often by formal religion. It's certainly impeded by conflicts between or among religions.

As I become more conscious, I think I see the important symbolism in the notion of reincarnation. In the West we take it literally—you die and you come back as a toad or something like that. It may well be literal, but that's not the point. It's really about the permanence of the spirit.

Another thing I hope for is a world where there's a lot less violence, where people are a lot healthier and experience less pain, and where they don't have so many physical disabilities.

Look at the ways in which Africa is basically coming apart as a result of colonial pressures and all the borders being fought over in the Congo and in Zimbabwe. At the same time AIDS and other diseases are rampant on that continent. And look at how the traditional tribal structures and the externally imposed colonial structures are breaking down. When you think about the fact that that's the cradle of civilization, that's where we all emerged from, you have to ask yourself a lot of questions.

A woman who just got back from Uganda was telling me, though, about all these local community organizations that are working. After the worst of what's happened in Uganda, and after all the deaths from religious cults, there are still people who are every day trying to construct a better world in those societies. So, am I going to see the macro-picture that looks utterly hopeless, or am I going to look at the micro-picture, where the human spirit is still very much alive? You can go anywhere—to the Balkans or to Austria—and see the tension between the emergence of a venomous, hateful philosophy and everyday people living their lives in positive and productive ways. They're good to their neighbors, and they have all the civic virtues we can think of.

I think at the macrolevel, things will continue to deteriorate. I don't think people in the Middle East are going to embrace one another. I think the Indians and the Pakistanis are not going to agree over Kashmir. But in each of those places there will continue to be people who say, "We've got to get up and go to work."

When will there be enough people working on those good things around the world that we reach a critical mass so that the trend turns positive? I'm optimistic that we'll tip the scale eventually, but it may be another thousand years.

It's easy to see how recent changes in communications could be for the worse. I mean, they often create the illusion that the individual can tailor, control, personalize, the medium. It gets prepackaged and sent to you in a way that feels personal. But you're really being manipulated by advertising in ways that are more profound now than ever. It just happens at a deeper, less obvious level.

When you think about these kids hacking into these fancy computers, the amazing thing is not that it happens but how few kids can actually do it. Every kid would like to do it, but it takes discipline, and you've got to be very smart.

My perfect world has a sun in it, I'm sure of that. And there's probably something that reminds us of our past, something ancient. It's a hospitable environment, so it has to have green. And it also has some blue water, kind of elemental. You know, the Garden of Eden was on the coast.

I guess you represent food with something that's growing on a tree, and it's abundant enough so that some of the fruit has fallen on the ground. In the corner there's a building, a little place to live, someplace simple, nothing grand. You know, in Turkey blue is a symbol of good luck, so the door is blue to ward off evil. But the house is made from earth. It reminds one of cultures that are past, and it looks a little Mediterranean. Certain places in Italy are amazing, where the ancient and the modern all come together, and the weather is nice all the time. So much depends on the light and the atmosphere. It's the kind of place that's imbued with a sense of both where we are and where we've been. (I've never done anything like this before.)

When the key to survival was brute force, the strongest survived. When the key became knowing how to hunt, you still had to be strong, but you also had to have the mechanical ability to make tools. Then the key to survival became being able to plant, so you needed to understand the forces of nature and seeds, which took a lot more discipline and patience. Well, we are now to the point where all the telecommunications stuff we're dealing with is approaching the complexity of our own intelligence. So, there will be very few people who know how to manipulate it. And that will change us for the worse. We'll be more and more directed by the technology. And it will become less and less a servant of ours.

I think the way we're going to survive as a race is that we'll have to go to Mars. If we stay here, we won't survive. Mars is just symbolic. We're going to go somewhere else so that we can perpetuate the spirit of renewal. If we don't, we'll do ourselves in, literally. We have to continue to reach out, continue to push.

May 3, 2000

Alan DERSHOWITZ

Felix Frankfurter Professor of Law, Harvard Law School; Attorney, Author, Civil Libertarian

Alan Dershowitz is the Felix Frankfurter Professor of Law at Harvard Law School and the author of more than a dozen books, including the best-selling *Chutzpah* (1991) and *Reversal of Fortune* (1996), which was made into an Academy Award–winning movie. Widely believed to possess one of the most brilliant legal minds in America, he was once described as "the top lawyer of last resort" for his legal defense of clients such as Anatoly Sharansky, Claus von Bülow, O. J. Simpson, and Michael Milken. He has also represented numerous impoverished and unknown defendants. Dershowitz lectures widely on both legal and Jewish topics.

Obviously, the most important things I might wish for the world are clichés, things that everybody wishes for: I want a world without war, without terrorism, without hate, without racism, without sexism, without homophobia. I want the value of human life to be respected much more than it is today. But those don't mark me as unique. Every good person from the beginning of history . . . The Jewish tradition for two thousand years or more has talked about swords being turned into plowshares. He who makes peace in his domain up in the heavens shall bring peace to earth. It's a prayer we've been saying for thousands of years, and I would like us to mean it.

I guess if I had one wish for the world today—and this is going to make my mother very unhappy—it is that we become less religious. I think religion has been a terrible, terrible innovation in the world in general. I think we needed it for years. But now I think people use religion, or God, as an excuse. There's a wonderful story about a Chassidic master who was asked: "Is there ever a place for atheism in the world?" And everybody expected him to say no. He said, "Yes, it's very important for you to act as an atheist in much of your life. You should always act as an atheist when anybody asks you for charity. Act as if God doesn't exist; act as if you're the only person who can help these people. You should always act as an atheist when it comes to dealings between you and other human beings. Don't blame God; don't expect God to step in." I wish we would learn that.

I'm not talking about whether people should believe in God or not, that's a personal choice.

I don't know how to draw it, but I'm thinking here of a world in which people maintain their differences but lower the walls and the barriers, a world in which people care about one another and live for this world, and not for some hereafter. A world in which people do good things because that's the right thing to do, not because God says to do it. What this is supposed to represent is different kinds of people all being equal, being tied together at the bottom, free to be different at the top, and being limited by the circle of the planet, in life here on Earth and not in some hereafter.

47

But institutional religion, as Thomas Jefferson recognized two hundred years ago, and as I think many people have recognized, has served as an excuse for so much harm in this world. Particularly religious fundamentalism. The blaming of God for all the good and bad things that happen in our society is the bane of modern civilization. And it's not only religion; it's spiritualism, irrationality, astrology. I want to get rid of spiritualism, the thought that things are beyond our control, out of our reach. The question is, are we strong enough to do that? Many people are not. Many people need the irrational in their life.

I don't mean to suggest that we shouldn't be warm and accepting and think that this mortal life and daily bread . . . There's much in religious tradition that is wonderful: the teachings of the prophets, the teachings of Jesus as a person, the teachings of some of the great religious leaders—as people—are wonderful. There is more to life than bread alone. But moving from there to the supernatural, using the supernatural as an excuse, is, I think, a terrible thing. I think it would be an interesting world without the supernatural.

Normally, when we try to eliminate the supernatural, some other autocracy takes over. Communism abolished God and instead made Stalin into God. That was not only not an improvement, it was a great step backward. God's better than Stalin because God isn't real and he doesn't kill people. Stalin was real and he killed people. So, I always tell terrorists and others: Pray for God to kill your enemies, fine, because it won't work. But don't kill them yourself.

Actually, there *is* room for spirituality in my conception, but it depends on how you define it. I'm a rational person who, I think, is spiritual. That is, I think there's more to life than the years that we're allotted here. I think we can hope to achieve things beyond the pragmatic. Love is spiritual. It's not particularly rational. Faith in humanity is spiritual. Hoping that we can do better than it looks like we can is spiritual. But I need a spirituality based in reason, not a spirituality based in giving up and letting someone else take over.

I can't stand ethicists who are buttinskis who tell me what I can do and what I can't do, tell me that fertility drugs are bad, or that organ donation has to be done in this way or that way. I think that most medical ethicists have no faith in human rationality, and they really believe in a kind of tyranny of the educated. I think most people are capable of making rational decisions. For example, once people are dead I don't think they own their organs. I would not allow a person to refuse to donate organs once they were dead. I think that substitutes faith in the irrational for the reality of life. If we could save another human being by taking out a dead person's kidneys or heart or lung, I think it's impermissibly selfish to forbid that because somehow you think that your heart goes with you into a world to come. Our bodies are on loan in some ways, and once life leaves them, I think, the organs belong to the future.

If I had one wish for the world it would be that we would stop blaming God, stop using God as an excuse, stop saying that God supports our views or opposes your views, that God is a member of our political party, that God believes in our country. If you need God, make him personal. Jesus was right when he talked about the hypocrites who pray at the door of the synagogues so that they can be seen. If you want to pray, pray in private. It's your freedom to do that. But it's very hard to think about religion. How do you think about an institution that has done so much good but that you are convinced is a pious fraud, as I am? It does a lot of good. It helps people die, believing there's a world to come. It helps people live in a world that doesn't give many of them much solace. It is pious, but it's also a fraud, and I think many religious people know that. That's the key.

I don't know what my own beliefs are at any given time. They always confuse me; I'm always in doubt, always questioning. Judaism has given me a lot. Mostly what it's given me is the ability to question everything. So I love Judaism. I hope Judaism continues. But Judaism transcends just religion. Some of the greatest Jews in his-tory have been secular Jews—Jews who had doubts about God, Jews who argued with God, Jews who refused to blame God. There are also secular Catholics, who doubt the theology but think the tradition is wonderful.

It doesn't mean that everything is black and white or everything is clear. We should acknowledge our doubts, acknowledge our uncertainties. We should acknowledge our lack of ability to understand. I don't think the human mind is capable of comprehending how we began. Surely mine is not. Maybe others are, but mine is not. I can't comprehend what was there before time. It's easy to fill that void with God. It's much more challenging to understand that we're just not capable of thinking about it. Ants are alive, and they're not capable of understanding the relationship between ants and human beings. Why should we be capable of understanding the relationship between ourselves and the deep-time beginnings of matter? It's just beyond our comprehension.   *November 25, 1997*

Michael DOMBECK

Chief, U.S. Forest Service (1997–2001)

Michael Dombeck served as chief of the U.S. Forest Service (Department of Agriculture) from 1997 to 2001. He is currently a professor of global environmental management at the University of Wisconsin. He was acting director of the Bureau of Land Management (Department of Interior) from 1994 to 1997.

One of the hallmarks of the United States is that land conservation is a core value here. The outdoors and open space are all part of our sense of basic freedom. The national Forest Service can take credit for a lot of programs that really do have a direct bearing on how close we come to our long-range view of a healthy, functioning world. A healthy ecosystem is measured in basic things like water quality and quantity, soil stability, the building of soils, the diversity of communities, those kinds of things. That's how you get resilience, the ability to deal with disasters. One thing I keep talking about is the importance of working within the limits of the land. Look, let's not be rigid in the way we apply various management practices. Let's let the land tell us in very simple terms what's good for us.

One of our scientists was telling me that in the eastern national forests we're rebuilding the soils that were degraded by clear-cuttings and burnings back in the 1800s and early 1900s. We need to continue to make that kind of progress. Most people don't think about soil health, but it's just as basic as making sure your temperature is 98.6 degrees, and your blood pressure is okay. The other part of an ideal world is water. It's as basic as soil. As a society we don't value water nearly as much as we should, or probably will fifty years from now.

Another thing I think about the United States, and I hope this doesn't sound egotistical, but it's a fact that anybody with average intelligence and a little bit of get-up-and-go can do okay. My

50

I guess I'll start this painting with a blue sky, puffy clouds, and a horizon. (I didn't know I was going to get to do fun stuff like this!) And my perfect world always has to have water in it, either a lake or a stream. And then, of course, we've got to have trees, different colored trees, different kinds. They don't all have to be evergreens. Here you've got open space. . . . I should have some wildlife in here.

life just exemplifies that. I often think about all the people lined up to immigrate into the United States, and how few want to leave.

The first time I went to a Third World nation, I came back feeling very strongly that as Americans we live in the best country from the standpoint of democracy and standard of living. I also felt that we're living in the best time ever from the standpoint of health, nutrition, longevity, conveniences, education, and the rest.

I grew up in northern Wisconsin, twenty-five miles from the nearest town of fifteen hundred. So I like the woods and feel very comfortable there. I can just close my eyes and smell the leaves lying on the ground. Those kinds of things are meaningful. I also grew up in a community of people who got along well together, and supported one another. In fact, we were focused on helping one another. So people are a very important part of any ideal world.

I've also had the great fortune of having some close friends who have stuck together, and a close family, and I think that's the thing I've gotten the most satisfaction from in my life. Material things you can lose or they can be stolen. But friendship and family bonds are something else.

In fact one thing I've come to appreciate more and more is the value of personal relationships and people just sitting and visiting with one another, versus the cold written word. As we get deeper and deeper into this age of computers, storytelling and verbal communication seem more and more important to me. I think if we did more of that as a society, there would be a lot more understanding. I hope the world doesn't get too impersonal.

In the world of natural resource management, I've seen a fair amount of disagreement. But one of the most rewarding things is when somehow, almost magically, people focus on common goals, and work together to achieve something that's in everybody's best interest.

The Wilderness Society and the National Cattlemen's Association are often at odds over grazing, and yet their most important value, and the common goal they should both be working toward, is open space. That's a core value, and when they see it, folks move forward out of the zone of controversy and into the zone of agreement, or at least partial agreement. Those of us who deal with forest health issues have to be more closely attuned to people. So much of what we deal with are social issues. In fact, forest health *is* a social issue.

August 5, 1997

James FALLOWS

Author; National Correspondent, The Atlantic Monthly; *Editor,* U.S. News & World Report *(1996–98)*

James Fallows is national correspondent for *The Atlantic Monthly* and the author of several books, including *Breaking the News* (1996) and *Free Flight: From Airline Hell to a New Age of Travel* (2001). Fallows served as editor of *U.S. News & World Report* for two years during the late 1990s and as President Carter's speechwriter during the first two years of that administration. Articles by Fallows on immigration, computer technology, defense policy, and economics have appeared in most major American magazines. He is also known for the several hundred commentaries he broadcast on NPR's *Morning Edition* during the 1980s and '90s.

I strongly believe that people are implanted early in their lives with a picture of a certain kind of geography. I grew up in southern California, and I love very much the sense of stark, open vistas, where you can see the geography and the geology. I feel sort of chronically ill at ease on the East Coast, where I've lived for the last twenty years.

Of course, I also liked very much being a foreign reporter in Japan and Malaysia and Burma. You walk around and everything you see is novel. So I would like a life in which I could just switch among these different kinds of environments.

I would certainly hope for a world that, in terms of the use of world resources, will reflect some better sense of sanity. Right now, you have the sense in Southeast Asia or South America of something like the great rape of the plains that happened a hundred years ago in the United States, but on a much larger scale. So I hope there will be some balance which keeps the world from becoming just one big urban environment.

I also would hope that, in industrialized countries, the trend toward things becoming more and more polarized economically will somehow be corrected. That seems to be the main side effect of this stage of world trade. I'd like that to be changed. I would hope that Africa and Latin America and the Middle East could have the same sense that, say, Southeast Asia has had in the last ten years—of people feeling like they're on the way up.

53

This is not an area of my brain that I normally call into play. Maybe I'll do this trick of drawing the world map and turning it upside down. I'll leave out great parts of the world's landmass, paint in these southern areas, and leave a hazy area for the United States and Europe. I want to imply the dark blue-black of the tropical forest region. These are the great granaries of the world. And this is the deep ecologic blue of the world's fisheries.

So here we have a representation of the forest regions, the grain-producing regions, and the fishery regions, which are the three things that are now endangered, all more or less stable. And then if we were to have centers of human possibility, we'd have to fill in a lot here in Japan and some in Korea, and some in Singapore, and up here in North America. So this is my representation of a perfect world in which crucial natural resources are preserved, and you have a much more broadly dispersed sense of people with hope and control over their lives.

54

I'd say that probably three-quarters to nine-tenths of the people alive today have their lives entirely constrained by the race in which they're born, the caste in which they're born, the country in which they're born—there are all these constraints. What each human being finally has is the number of years he or she is alive on Earth, and most people have no choice about how that is spent, because of these constraints. So expanding the proportion of people who have some control over their lives, that would be what I would hope for.

Also, if I knew there was a way to eliminate, in the short run, all the problems of gasoline—having to find gasoline, to burn gasoline, to transport gasoline, to worry about carbon dioxide and nuclear power—that is another thing I would wish for. I think solar energy is the single most immediate panacea to a whole range of world problems that one could imagine. I know there are side effects of not using oil and coal, but I would argue that on a world scale those are small compared to the problems of using fossil fuels.

Things usually turn out neither as well as they could nor as badly as we fear at any given time. I mean, there are exceptions in world history where things really became disastrous—World War II and Nazism, for example, World War I and the complete destruction of the old European order. But I would argue that those have been the exceptions. Over the last thirty-five years many things have gone much less badly than most people expected. We have not had nuclear war. There have not been widespread worldwide famines. Environmental destruction has not been as bad as people feared twenty years ago. The Koreas have not gone to war with each other, and AIDS has not devastated the whole world population. I suppose I am modestly optimistic that, as emergencies come, they will be averted, for self-preservation reasons. There is an animal cunning in the human species—some adaptive behavior—that allows us to survive.

March 3, 1997

Anita PEREZ FERGUSON

Director, InterAmerican Foundation (since 2000);
President, National Women's Political Caucus
(1996–99)

Anita Perez Ferguson is a director for the InterAmerican Foundation in Washington, D.C., and a visiting lecturer for the Woodrow Wilson Foundation in Princeton, New Jersey. Perez Ferguson formerly served as president of the National Women's Political Caucus, and before that as White House liaison to the U.S. Department of Transportation. She is the author of *A Passion for Politics* (1999) and coauthor of *Women Seen and Heard* (2001). She was named among the One Hundred Most Influential Hispanics in the United States by *Hispanic Business* magazine.

What I would hope for is that more people would feel more enabled to participate in shaping their destiny. My biggest concern with our democracy and with the political and social situation of people around the world is not so much that people are frequently in need, or oppressed, it's that they are without the power, or feel they are without the power, to change their circumstance. I think a tremendous difference can be made with grassroots efforts: politically, spiritually, and economically.

More women will certainly continue to take their place among the decision makers of the world, in politics, in business, and in every aspect of our lives. And this will indeed be a change from what we've known historically. Whether or not as these women arrive in positions of leadership they maintain the characteristics we now see among women in general—a more cooperative spirit, less antagonistic, more collaborative styles—whether that is maintained, and begins to permeate the geopolitical systems of the world, remains to be seen. The reverse might also happen—that the established geopolitical systems, heavily divided by nation-states, very conflict-oriented, very scarce-resource-oriented, may overtake those women and change them. We can only hope for the best.

I just returned from the east coast of Africa, where I was doing leadership training for women. I've also taught women in South America, in Argentina, and I've traveled a good deal. The issues I deal with are global in scope, and I enjoy making application of them to women, even outside the United States.

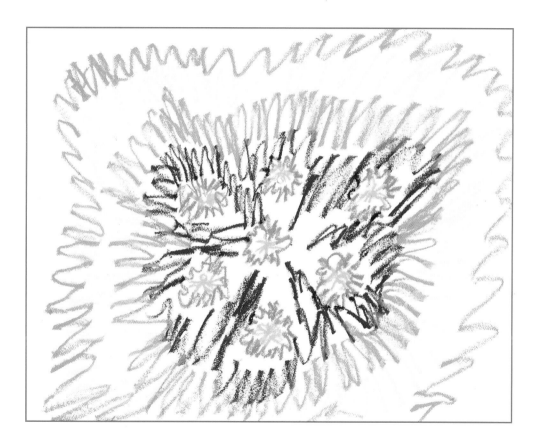

What I'm thinking of in this painting is that there's a lot of life around, and that life as it grows relates to everything else, not only on Earth but actually further into a spiritual type of relation. So I'm just going to put in the pieces of life—light green, like a new leaf, and darker green. And some of it is the plants and animals and what we know on Earth, but there's probably a lot more universally that we don't know about yet, not necessarily on Earth. So I'm going out from the green, which I see as the life we're aware of (the dark green might be more maturity in that), going beyond that to what might be a creator or a higher form. And I think that's really where we are in our best consciousness.

Another thing I would hope for in an ideal world would be that we all appreciate better our real spiritual connection to the other things and creatures we share this planet with. I think the whole system of creation, our connection with much larger forces, is something that we're just now starting to explore, in terms of the origins of our universe, and the origins of plant and animal life. We've got a lot more connecting to do intellectually, philosophically, and spiritually.

If we look at all the species that we know of now and those that we have historical evidence of, we're all dependent on one another. As human beings, we haven't taken that too seriously. But we can obviously see, from the air we breathe to the water we drink, to where many of our medicinal components come from, that we are connected to one another. Whether we feel that some bark on a tree in South America relates to us or not, all of us melt down to certain basic elements that can be, and should be, compatible.

What I mean by *spirituality* is what we look like on the inside, not just in our own capsulated bodies but also how we connect with other people. I might connect to all Hispanics, or to all people with certain physical characteristics or similar beliefs. In the same way we connect in our beliefs and in our experiences and emotions with our ancestors, with our parents, with our grandparents, and with those historically who have shared our beliefs.

It's possible for us to be inspired by someone who lived decades ahead of us, who's not a relation in any way. They put into our spirit a certain idea or way of thinking, and that goes all the way back to the origin of creation and what I call God. We have the capability of connecting to our Creator by understanding more about the universe around us, and being more in tune with it. So spirituality is how we connect with humankind before us, all the way back to the creation.

I'm definitely a water person. I would identify with a sea otter, a creature that has great mobility in distance, because of the interconnectedness of our oceans, and also great flexibility in terms of depth. With that depth it gets into many different environmental strata—close to the surface and down to the bottom of the sea. So, the variety, the fluidity, the mobility, remind me of what I do in my life—moving from group to group, country to country, across ethnic lines, racial lines, gender lines.   *May 2, 1997*

Kathryn FULLER

President, World Wildlife Fund (since 1989)

Kathryn Fuller became president and CEO of World Wildlife Fund (WWF) in 1989. She served previously as that organization's executive vice president, general counsel, and director of public policy and wildlife trade monitoring programs. Her tenure at WWF has been characterized by innovative conservation methods, and she is credited with having doubled the membership and tripled the revenues of the organization. Before joining WWF in 1983, Fuller practiced law with the U.S. Department of Justice, where she headed the Wildlife and Marine Resources Section of the Land and Natural Resources Division.

I want to see measurable progress in achieving conservation protection in several key ecoregions: the Bering Sea, the remnants of tall grass prairie, the Everglades, the great swamps, the Congo forests, the Amazon forests, and so forth. We don't want to focus just on species numbers, or species diversity, but really on distinctive ecological regions.

It's important to declare new parks, manage endangered species, and convince multinationals not to pursue certain kinds of resource exploitation. And then there are the overarching threats: human population growth at the top of the list, along with human consumption patterns.

So while our direct goal may not be to address human population pressure, nonetheless we have to do it. If the goal is to make the world a living planet for future generations, as we say, the necessary corollary to that is for people to live in a sustainable way. We cannot be consuming resources at the rate we do. We have to find better models to shape markets. This is real, and everyone should care about it.

A lot of what we do is premised on involving local populations. Unless the people who live in and around important populations of wildlife have a direct stake in the conservation of those animals, we won't succeed. One step might be to reopen a wildlife park for use by the local communities during a specified period. Then the communities see that their economic and social prosperity is linked to the park, and they become the most dedicated conservationists of the park. Or we find

59

out that a local community has problems with rhinos raiding crops. Well, they can dig a ditch around the garden, put boards across it that people can walk across but rhinos won't. The real-world consequence of a modest, low-tech solution like that might be that the rhino population grows from, say, forty animals to over four hundred. So understanding the needs of the people is critical.

Another critical thing is the role of women as stewards of natural resources, and seeing women become full participants in community decision making. Women do most of the world's farming, and most of the world's work. In rural areas women are most involved with the land and wildlife day to day. They're also typically willing to make sound decisions for the future because, more than men, women take a long view. They really are looking out for their children and grandchildren. But so far women haven't had the tools, the education, the social status, and so forth.

So we're really promoting a number of things: women's education, open civil societies, more equal distribution of the world's resources. And those larger agendas are more achievable if women play a more central role.

As I get older I have an increasingly keen appreciation for how important it is to celebrate when things are going well. I see so many people whose circumstances are much more difficult than mine, so I'm enormously grateful that I have what by any measure would be a pretty good deal in life.

The World Wildlife Fund has been a successful organization in terms of conservation achievements in its thirty-five-year history. But, while we may be winning some battles, by any objective measure we're losing the war. I believe in the resilience of the planet and the resilience of the human spirit, but it's hard not to be discouraged when you look at any number of indicators: human population growth, carbon emissions, fisheries depletion, forest depletion, water scarcity, water quality, erosion, contamination from organic chemicals, and so forth.

It's a challenge to persuade people that not only are these issues real and important, but they're also not hopeless. We all can make a difference. If people don't understand that we're all just pieces of the puzzle, then we won't succeed.   *May 28, 1997*

The notion in this painting is that we have our planet with its thin layer of atmosphere, which we need. Then we have deserts, tundra, deciduous forests, wetlands, river systems, and so forth. This is Australia with the forests of northern Queensland. Here you have boreal forests and pack ice across the Bering Strait. Now, I'll add different plants and animals and people around the sides: a butterfly here and another further up, to suggest the inter-connectedness and migratory nature of these animals. They have to move. Then maybe with the notion of the living planet I'll connect them in ways that suggest that we need func-tioning, unbroken linkages. The basic systems intact.

61

$Arun$ GANDHI

Cofounder and President, M. K. Gandhi Institute for Nonviolence (since 1991)

Arun Gandhi cofounded (with his wife) the M. K. Gandhi Institute for Nonviolence in Memphis, Tennessee, named after Arun's grandfather, the great spiritual leader Mahatma Gandhi. The institute's mission is to promote the principles of nonviolence through workshops, seminars, and community service. Gandhi previously founded India's Center for Social Unity, which has helped mitigate poverty and caste discrimination among more than 500,000 rural Indians living in over three hundred Indian villages. He is also the author of eight books and hundreds of articles.

The environment I personally thrive in is one where there is peace and harmony. We have tried to create that, and I think very substantially we have succeeded. Conflict is always there. It's a part of life. And whenever there's a major conflict, we sit across the table and discuss how best we can resolve it. More often than not I think we've been able to resolve the conflict to the satisfaction of both sides.

What happens in normal circumstances is that tempers are lost, people say things in anger, and it keeps escalating, because the other person responds in anger, too. So, before you know it, finding a solution becomes very difficult.

One thing we have tried to do in our work is to make people understand that anger is a very good emotion that drives us. But how we use that energy is what we need to concentrate on, because we have not been taught about that. When we abuse the energy of anger, we become very negative. But if we learn that anger is good and powerful, it is just as powerful and deadly as electricity, and also just as useful. So we have to learn to use it respectfully and intelligently, to channel anger into positive action. That's one of the most important lessons for all human beings, which many people have ignored.

In our systems, anger is the trip switch that tells us something is wrong in the circuit, things are getting out of hand. But instead of using anger intelligently as a trip switch and with a calm mind

In this painting I'm trying to create a peaceful feeling, which I've always found on the seashore, enjoying the quiet and peaceful tropical beach. I don't know if I'll be able to do it well. I'm thinking specifically of a lovely sitting beach in Maui, where I went last August. I would like to draw human beings, swimming and just having fun, but I am just awful at them.

63

trying to find a proper solution to the problem, we often lash out and say and do things that we later regret.

One thing I'm hoping for is this peaceful harmony I mentioned. The twentieth century has been the most violent century in history, and that is not something we can be proud of. I do believe that we as human beings can make this a more peaceful world if each of us attempts to do that. So, in the footsteps of my grandfather, I can plant seeds in the minds of people and hope those seeds germinate.

Another priority of mine is to alleviate the poverty in many parts of the world, and to rebuild the self-respect and self-confidence of poor people. Poor people all over the world suffer tremendously, first because of poverty, and secondly because more affluent people feed them, clothe them, and give them charity, which crushes them more. They come to feel that they cannot do anything for themselves, that they are useless. So they lose their self-respect and self-confidence.

If a person were hungry, then talking to that person about peace and harmony would be useless. The economy is the first thing that gives a person stability, though that doesn't mean we have to follow the present pattern of economic development, which is very self-oriented and selfish. Capitalism means amassing things for yourself. In our capitalistic and materialistic society, people don't matter. Profits matter, and that's a tragedy. Profits should be secondary. People should be the most important thing.

I am not saying that we don't need capitalism. We do need it, but we need compassionate capitalism, where the wealth is spread out. Of course, the democracy that we have today is not a perfect system either. We need to perfect it, and we need to devote some time to this. It is not going to perfect itself.

I lived in the city of Bombay for thirty years, and Bombay has a tremendous number of homeless people, not only because of the high birth rate but also because Bombay is the concentration of wealth. So that wealth attracts poor people. Everybody wants to survive, and they feel that if they go to Bombay, even if they don't get a job, they can beg for food, and somebody will give it to them. There is a continuous influx, and the city gets choked, with all the civic amenities breaking down. Everybody is screaming for help and nobody knows what to do.

So my friends and I decided to use my grandfather's concept of trusteeship and constructive action. Grandfather said that each one of us has a talent, but that we don't own our talent. We are trustees of it, and as trustees of our talents we should use them for other people as much as we use them for ourselves. That leads to constructive action.

So we brought together about six hundred homeless people and challenged them to save a coin every day. Now at first this seemed ridiculous. How can you expect homeless people who don't know where their next meal is coming from to save a coin every day? But we wanted them to be a part of the solution. We could have gone to somebody rich and gotten the money to create an economic infrastructure, and that would have been faster. But that would have given them the impression that they could ask for whatever they wanted, and people would produce it. That is not what we wanted them to feel. So we told them we didn't know how they were going to do this. "You may have to work extra hard, or you may have to cut back on something you eat or smoke. You decide personally how you're going to do it." They took up that challenge and within about eighteen to nineteen months they came back to us with the equivalent of $11,000.

So with that money we bought them ten secondhand textile machines and installed those machines in a little tin shed in one of their villages. Now they didn't know money management or marketing, so we trained them in these things. And as they became confi-dent, we handed the responsibility to them. They worked day and night, and made that factory a tremendous success. And today they have four factories with more than seven hundred machines. And all the people who contributed to the fund are now back in their villages living a much more decent life, earning more money, sending their kids to schools. They also have continued with that small savings habit, and in 1978 they opened their first cooperative bank in Bombay. Now that bank has seven branch offices, with total assets worth nearly $2 million.

What we did was not a major sacrifice. We were ordinary people. All we sacrificed was our free time. Every moment we had, we spent with these people advising them, and it was much more fulfilling than spending our vacation time skiing or just enjoying ourselves. We proved that it is possible to do this.   *November 16, 2000*

Kim GANDY

*President, National Organization for Women
(since 2001)*

66

Kim Gandy succeeded Patricia Ireland as president of the National Organization for Women (NOW) in the summer of 2001, after having served as executive vice president of that organization since 1991. She was an active member of the drafting committees for the 1991 Civil Rights Act, which entitled women to a jury trial in cases of sex discrimination and harassment, and the Freedom of Access to Clinic Entrances Act, which reduced the violence at clinics that provide abortion.

I hope for myself and for my two daughters that women will finally get equal rights and equal opportunities, not just in the United States but all over the world. In this country I also hope that we'll finally get women in the United States Constitution. I am passionate about that issue.

I sometimes hear people say that women have already achieved equality in the United States. Well, those people clearly haven't been paying attention. In the United States women are still paid less than men for similar work. Overall, women earn seventy-four cents compared to a dollar earned by men for full-time, year-round work. Women of color, even less than that.

We're also still the primary providers of both child care and elder care, for which we get punished in many ways. One example is that the Social Security system treats as a zero any year that you're out of the workforce for caregiving, so that those years drop out of any calculation of your Social Security benefits. So not only are women expected to be the primary caregivers, but they suffer losses in benefits and other advantages as a result of their caregiving, which is not recognized as work.

There is also really no provision for child care in this country, which disadvantages women much more than it does men. Women are also disproportionately the victims of sexual assault and sexual violence in society. Approximately one in five girls have been victims of sexual assault. So the list is long. Our reproductive rights are constantly in jeopardy. We're going backwards on issue after issue, not just abortion rights but also birth control. The right wing had ignored birth control for a

This is a painting of a bunch of people. You can't really tell whether they're men or women. They're both. And it's as though you're looking from above at a group of people in a circle, who are all holding hands and bowing to each other respectfully. I tried to make them different sizes, because some of them are supposed to be children. People of all races. My artistic abilities are severely lacking, but that's close enough.

67

long time and only went after abortion rights, but now they're going after birth control as well. There are all kinds of ways, small and large, that our reproductive freedoms are being reduced.

I spent most of my adult life in New Orleans. And on my first job after law school there, I had my very first experience with laws that discriminated against women. I was a new employee and was filling out the form for the employee stock option plan. At the end it said, "If a married woman, husband must sign here." So I asked my boss what that meant. And he said, "Oh, that's the head and master law. It just means that your husband owns your paycheck." Now I was not especially world-wise at the time, but there was definitely something about this that was just not quite right.

So I showed up at the next meeting of the local NOW chapter and said, "Here I am, and I'm going to get rid of this head and master thing," which I spent the next seven years doing. That one experience of having to hand my husband this card to sign in order for me to benefit from my own paycheck was what got me started.

I am guardedly optimistic, though. I think there will be a lot of damage done to women's rights during the next three years. But I also think we'll be successful at getting the message out to women and men who care about these issues before too many of them have personal tragedies as a result of this administration's policies. I plan personally to continue working for justice for women and girls. And when we do finally have a just world, then what I want to do is retire and grow roses.

August 22, 2001

Candace GINGRICH

Manager, National Coming Out Project, Human Rights Campaign (since 1998)

Candace Gingrich is manager of the National Coming Out Project of the Human Rights Campaign, the largest lesbian and gay political organization in the country. She lobbies Congress, coordinates campaign support, and educates the public on gay and lesbian issues, using the name recognition afforded by her brother, Newt Gingrich, who became Speaker of the U.S. House of Representatives in 1995. Candace Gingrich is the author of *The Accidental Activist* (1996).

I hope we'll all advance in equality and see an end to the "isms," whether sexism or racism or heterosexism. If we work toward federal legislation to stop discrimination, that's really just treating the symptoms. The cure is reaching out to people to help them see that gay and lesbian people are their neighbors and their co-workers and their friends. I hope for a world where people (a) understand their common humanity, and (b) recognize that the discrimination that gay, lesbian, and bi- and trans- people face is wrong and should be stopped.

I actually think that most people are guilty of stereotyping in one way or another, and I'm not any different from the next person. But I would hope that most of the time I'm able to recognize that that's what I'm doing.

The biggest life change for me happened when my brother became Speaker of the House. Before that, I lived a sheltered life. I had never been fired from a job because I was gay, and I didn't know anybody who had been. I also didn't know anybody who was a victim of a hate crime. I didn't even know anybody with AIDS or HIV. But suddenly I was fortunate to be able to reach a large audience and, hopefully, effect change. Actually, everybody can effect change, even if it's glacial. It may be just encouraging people to register to vote, and then voting. Or it may be coming out to your family or deciding to do Habitat for Humanity, or deciding to take the subway instead of your car.

Gay and lesbian issues are very specific to the country you're in. The lives of gay people in the

69

Great color selection! How cool! This painting is about the interconnectedness of it all. On the global level, we're all connected. The bombing runs we do on Puerto Rico affect the fish and the water, and that affects people. Cutting all the shade trees in South America so that the coffee grows faster means fewer nesting places for the migrant birds, and that means that there won't be many of those birds coming to America. Everything's connected. Injustice anywhere is a threat to justice everywhere. We're all in this together, and we will all be better served if we recognize that.

United States are quite different than in, say, Jamaica, where the government says homosexuals should be killed and they have been in the past. Different also than in Denmark, where they're recognized as full and equal citizens, with the right to marry. So it's varied. But environmental issues are much more universal.

Much of my work has been gay activism, but underneath all that I'm really worried about whether we'll even have an Earth to be equal in. I hope the people in control will realize that global warming is a real problem, so that we won't have the Far East overcome by sludge from melting glaciers. I hope we realize that much of the problem is produced right here in our own country with our vehicles.

I guess global warming for me is the most recent problem I've been outraged about because there are still people in positions of power who ignore it. It's so unfair, because the United States is making global warming happen, and the most dire consequences are going to be felt in the Third World. The big floods and waves are going to happen in India and Hong Kong. I really don't want to be around for the end of the world knowing that it was something we could have avoided. That would really piss me off.

I also hate sprawl. Being a bird-watcher, I know that what's happening in South America affects what happens here in the States with migration. My partner is a nature writer, and she always says there's no such thing as private property. In dozens of ways the things we do (deciding whether to put insecticide on our lawns, or whether we should mulch) affect everyone else because those chemicals run off into the bay, or they kill the spiders that eat the mosquitoes. Everything is connected. It's all related.

It may be your choice to drive your '78 LTD and spew however much stuff out the back, but it affects all kinds of other things. Discriminating against somebody because of the color of their skin could quite possibly affect their ability to put a roof over their head or feed their children. And that's going to have an effect on society as a whole, because if they become throwaway people, we'll need to create programs to help them. The Golden Rule applies not just to people but also to how we treat the earth and the sky, and the water. Whether it's in the workplace or the courts or wherever, you have to have a level playing field. It's hard, but it's the right thing to do. The gap between rich and poor doesn't just affect the poor. People need to take responsibility for what they're capable of giving.   *January 24, 2001*

$\mathcal{D}aniel$ GOLDIN

Chief Administrator, NASA (1992–2001)

72

Daniel Goldin served as chief administrator of NASA for nine years, beginning in 1992. Using the motto "better, cheaper, faster," he streamlined and restructured major programs. He was successful at pulling NASA out of its Cold War mentality and promoting cooperative endeavors, including the International Space Station, with the Russian Space Agency. Other NASA successes during Goldin's tenure included the repair of the Hubble Space Telescope and the successful launch of the Mars Pathfinder mission.

I hope for a world in which we have come to our senses, and children do not have to live in fear of weapons of mass destruction. Fear causes deviant behavior.

The next thing I wish for is a society in which gender and culture and race do not cause the dashing of hopes for young people. I'd like opportunity not to know bounds by race, or culture, or gender.

The third thing I hope for is that the young people of this country will always be able to have the same dreams and hopes that I had in the 1950s. That was a decade of incredible excitement in this country. Parents knew their children would have a better life than they did; children knew there were tremendous possibilities for them. There seemed to be no limits, no stops.

And finally, in this perfect world, the driving force for all of this will be unbelievable technological achievements that will allow people to live healthier, fuller lives with economic opportunity—technologies that provide energy and products of economic value without consuming valuable resources or spewing poisons into the air. *Sustainable development* is the term I prefer.

There are two cultures in the world, those who look up and those who look down. Those who look down know with certainty what can't be done. Those who look down know that there's only disaster ahead. I'm one who looks up, and I believe that this human species is going to perpetuate itself through space. Ultimately we're going to leave planet Earth.

I don't know that it relates to what I said, but I do know what I want to draw. I would say the last time I did this was maybe kindergarten or first grade. There's the final frontier! There's the ocean; there's the land. (The brown represents the land.) And at the center of our own planet, there's a hot core. Now here's a rocket with a nice rocket trail. These are supposed to be the suns, and I put lots of planets around them. Now these are very happy planets, because they don't have any responsibility. I wanted to show that there are loads of other worlds out there, dead worlds and live worlds.

As people left Europe to come to a new world, as they left Polynesia to populate the Pacific, there was opportunity. I'd like to know that there's opportunity out there, too. And I'd like future children to be able to take that trip and open the frontier to create opportunities. And then we continue the expansion. That is my philosophy of life. And that is why I have to pinch myself to know that I have this job. I mean, every day I have to thank the president for allowing me to do this.

I'll tell you a story. I went to my daughter's class when she was in the second or third grade to talk to them about how the solar system formed, how the planets formed, how life began. And then I told them that the sun was going to burn out in about five billion years. And the children who look up got hysterical! Now that is the ultimate in positive attitude! They were running around crying, "The sun's going to burn out. Oh my God!"

Now, the point is, nothing is given forever. Clearly, belief in God and religion enter into this, and I can't give you the intersection between theology and science. But what I can tell you is that this human species is going to leave this planet and explore the heavens. There's no doubt in my mind. It's our ultimate fate. The human species needs new frontiers.

It's very hard being lonely. We all at some point in our lives have had these debates in our heads, some more so than others. I know in my case I struggle a lot with God and my belief in God and the reason for life. And I'd like to know that there are other life-forms, even if they're just bacteria. I don't need the little green men.

If there were no other life-forms, it would be like being completely alone. I don't know how many billions and trillions of planets there are. But if in this entire universe (and there's some belief that there may be other universes, too), but if in billions of bodies,

there's only one place where there's life. . . . If it's God's will, so be it. But it would be nice to believe that there's life elsewhere. It's hard to imagine that life has taken place on just this one planetary body, which has a finite life measured in geological time. It would be nice to know that life is ubiquitous. It's a necessity for an optimist.

I can't speak to what might be God's will. I don't know. But I once went hiking with four or five of my friends, and we got up to the top of this mountain, Mt. Whitney, really early—two or three in the afternoon. So everyone went to sleep. I said, "You're crazy, you'll wake up in the middle of the night and be uncomfortable." So I went away from them, and by myself I watched the sun set, and the moon and stars come out. And then I had a really scary experience. I started shivering. As I lay there, I thought about the vastness of space and time and here I am on this little, itty-bitty spot for a flash in time. Earth has been here 4.6 billion years, and I don't know how many more billions of years it's going to exist, and I'm here for this short time span. So I got scared. I looked out into the vastness of space and said, "What is the meaning of life?" I need God to help me understand this. It was very scary. And then I also thought about how important it would be to know that life could take shape in other places, too, so that we won't be alone. So there's hope.

June 9, 1997

Bernadine HEALY

President and CEO, American Red Cross (1999–2001); Dean, College of Medicine and Public Health, Ohio State University (1995–99); Director, National Institutes of Health (1991–93)

Bernadine Healy served as president and CEO of the American Red Cross for two years beginning in 1999. She was dean of the College of Medicine and Public Health at Ohio State University from 1995 to 1999. Before that, she served as the first female director of the National Institutes of Health (NIH), where she managed nineteen thousand employees and an annual budget of over $11 billion. At the NIH, Healy launched the $625 million Women's Health Initiative. During the Reagan administration, she served as deputy director of the Office of Science and Technology Policy.

I have no doubt that this planet will be here in fifty years, but I certainly hope that it will not have been touched in any major way by weapons of mass destruction. With the proliferation of terrorism that we're seeing now, there are real concerns about these weapons being in the hands of people with no allegiance to international law, and without any recognition of the need to protect human life, even their own. I want a world that has been spared from that kind of threat.

I also hope for a world in which this really phenomenal informational technology that we're developing now, the megamind that's being created in computers and supersupercomputers, is used to benefit the planet, not to control the planet. No doubt, some of these computers can exceed the human mind in terms of the number of interactions or connections they make. Yet that mastermind might indeed be schizophrenic, since it would lack the pruning that occurs naturally in the human brain through pressures from society and human values.

One would hope for a world in which these extraordinary computers are used to enable people to perhaps get over differences, to communicate in ways that lead to the same goodness that comes out so often when people face each other and recognize the humanity in each other.

As a physician, as a scientist, I've often challenged the Luddites who say stop to new technologies. But I do have a concern. It's a question of governance. Have we become so confident that science will do good, because it's done so much good in the past, that we now take for granted that it will always do good?

This painting is very simple, a red cross. You know, the red cross is actually five squares. People think it's a cross, a religious symbol, but it's not. The red cross was never intended to be a religious symbol. It was the reverse of the Swiss flag in part, which represents neutrality. I had the head of our archives go back and get me the historical meaning of the five squares, so I can give them to you. I mean, they're beautiful. This goes back to the 1920s. Here it is: love (the love of humanity); hope (for those in distress); tradition (the glorious history of the movement); faith (confidence in the organization, but faith in one another, faith in the ideal world); and service. So it's very simple and elegant and beautiful. The five squares.

76

I hope that with respect to advanced molecular biology, the manipulation of genomes and cloning, that this is a world in which fundamental moral and ethical principles overlie these powerful technologies. This is a world in which people are healthier, better educated, and more in control of themselves. Where people have freedoms but adhere to common humanitarian values.

Actually, anybody's perfect world is the world they have in their most immediate environment. It's in the relationships you have, and the ways you've nurtured them throughout your lifetime. Of course that includes, hopefully, your family, the generation past and future, your parents, your children, your spouse. That's the most critical part of anybody's ideal world, and that ideal world hasn't really changed over centuries. If you read great literature, the Bible, the psalms, you'll see that humans haven't changed fundamentally, worrying about their children, their parents, their inner souls, their relationships. That's what it's all about.

I think the aspiration toward an ideal world has always been centered in the soul and in the human heart. But I do think we can fulfill that better now than we could a hundred years ago, or five hundred years ago, or two thousand years ago. I mean, look at the role of women. Women are now in a much better position than they ever were to care for their children, to relate to their spouses in positive ways. Of course, there are parts of the world in which women are still exactly where they were five hundred years ago. But certainly in our society, we are every year approaching closer to that

ideal world, a better quality of life in a very personal sense. I guess my sense of an ideal world is one in which your immediate sphere is filled with rich human relationships, the whole family living around you. Maybe that would be ideal. (Maybe it wouldn't.) I believe in extended families.

That's come from my life in medicine. I know that when people are facing their last moments of life, they are not thinking about the money they made, or the degrees they have, or the fame they've achieved. They're thinking about the people they love, and the people who love them. It becomes this intimate circle, their ideal world, the best measure of their life.

Now, the society you live in, the kind of government and economic system you live under, the human rights laws that apply, whether you have a bill of rights or a constitution, whether there's freedom of speech—all those things are enablers. It's very hard for anyone to even imagine an ideal world when they can't feed their children. And, obviously, physical health is an enabler, too. And class. There always will be some range of God-given talent, and some range of economic fulfillment. But you can't have that too broad, and you particularly can't make that capricious.

Our spirits, our aspirations, our dreams, aren't very different from what people wanted one hundred years ago. But this modern world has enabled us to achieve our ideals. If you look back to the Middle Ages, life was cheap, and that's just not the case anymore. An ideal world is a world in which life is not cheap.

This morning I jotted down what I consider an ideal environment for the Red Cross, but I think it applies for anyone. The first thing is that we all have a common mission. That's true in your home or your work. You have to share a mission, and hopefully that mission will be noble. You're not just there; you believe in something that goes beyond yourself.

Second, work is critically important, because it's part of developing who we are. An ideal world is one in which work brings out the essence of who you are, brings out your full life, fulfillment. We hear about an ideal world in which we can play more and work less. To the contrary. So I think it would mean having a noble work ethic, so that you really can believe that your labor creates something that gets beyond yourself.

Respect. I want a world in which people respect one another because of their unique talents. I mean, that's obvious. We say it a lot. But I worry that we're becoming more and more Balkanized, not more and more respectful, even in our own country.

I think interdependence (you know, "No man is an island") with people who aren't necessarily just like you. Interdependence within a community, within a family, country to country. Ultimately, an ideal world is one based on trust and integrity, just like in human relationships.

I hope also for a world that has some sense of what's good and bad, right and wrong. Sometimes I worry we're allowing that to blur. I mean, do we have shared expectations or does everybody's private ethics cancel out? I personally believe that certain things are crisp. Not a lot of things, but certain things are not relative. These are on the tablets. You know, the Ten Commandments aren't really terrible. I don't care whether it was Moses or the man next door. There is an immutable dimension there. You don't kill. You don't steal. It's all about relationships. Everything in the Ten Commandments is about how humans should interact, and there are some dos and don'ts.

I also think it should be a world in which we celebrate real heroes, not just celebrities. My ideal world would be one in which we celebrate the people who've really done the noble things.

August 28, 2001

John HENDRICKS

Founder, Chairman, and CEO, Discovery Communications, Inc. (since 1985)

John Hendricks is founder, chairman, and CEO of Discovery Communications, Inc., a global media empire with cable networks (including the Discovery Channel, the Learning Channel, and Animal Planet) that are seen in at least 155 countries and territories by an estimated 425 million viewers. Discovery Communications also operates 165 retail stores in the United States alone. Hendricks worked previously as an administrator at the University of Alabama.

My most fundamental hope is for a worldwide attitude of tolerance, which I think will only come through education and an awareness of other cultures and religions. The more people are exposed to other philosophies and thought, the more possible it becomes to resolve world conflicts peacefully. Education builds tolerance for other points of view.

I also think media can be key to breaking down barriers worldwide, because they have such a huge potential to penetrate. If media are used to educate and enlighten, one outcome will be tolerance, and human beings will advance over time.

I love to sit down at night and watch one of the network news shows, because they're attempting to tell you everything that's happening in the world in thirty minutes. Dan Rather or Peter Jennings or Tom Brokaw is saying, "Of all the stuff that's happening in the world, here're the few things that we think you should know." And so, by boiling it down, they make a presentation that the community of citizens can witness. That's the important role of news editorials, and the news is one of the few places where people everywhere can share a common knowledge of what's happening.

My career has been about advanced media that employ educational content that improves the human condition. I'm proud that the Discovery Channel is now being broadcast into 155 other countries and territories. I think we've been so successful because people have a very fundamental natural curiosity. Sometimes we all just want to laugh and be amused by television, and that's entertainment, but we develop our service for people when they're in their curious mode.

Personally, I'm very attracted to fundamental questions. Why is there something rather than nothing? Why is there all this stuff, and how did it happen? Stephen Hawking and other physicists can take you down to the early milliseconds after the big bang, but how does something spring out of nothing? Some physicists would say that's a meaningless question.

Is life unique to Earth, or has it happened elsewhere? If it's happened just once in our solar system, then the chances are that just millions of other life-starts have happened in the universe. Right now we have only this one event, so we can't do the statistics. But if we could verify that life had occurred someplace else, then we could. To me it seems so profound. We may be the last generation born with knowledge of only life here on Earth. And we might die with the knowledge that there's life elsewhere.

If a chain of elements, atoms and molecules, elsewhere did this marvelous trick of aligning itself in a pattern that can replicate itself so perfectly that its ability to replicate itself could also be passed on, then that's the beginning of life. It would be hard to get to a point, at least in our lifetime, when we could say we know we're it, and we're the only it. I mean, how could we ever prove that? It's more likely that there's life elsewhere, and that has enormous significance to me. We may have thought we were precious before, but if we're the only it, then our lives truly are precious.

I'm very aware right now that the duration of our lives is very short. So in my perfect world I also want to see some cures for some of the awful diseases out there, like cancer. Those problems are solvable, and I'm convinced that in ten years or thirty years diseases like that will be things of the past. *May 23, 1997*

My picture of an ideal world has to include people, so this painting is about civilization as well as nature. The blue is for clean water and sky. But there's also an artificial path. People are in this natural world, along with animals. And someone is reading or just contemplating something under a tree. Many times I've sat back up against a tree in the grass, and that's just ideal for me. That's my ideal world!

81

Dudley HERSCHBACH

Nobel Laureate (Chemistry, 1986); Baird Professor of Science, Harvard University

Dudley Herschbach is the Baird Professor of Science at Harvard University, where he has taught since 1963. In 1986 he won the Nobel Prize in chemistry for his development of techniques to study the motion of molecules during collisions. In 1991 he was awarded the National Medal of Science. He is also a Fellow of the American Academy of Arts and Sciences and the National Academy of Sciences.

The thing I get the biggest kick out of personally is working with students. I love figuring out things, which is what research and teaching are. In science you don't do research alone. You might come in with an idea that you tell a student about, and then they get excited. And then you realize you overlooked something that maybe the student discovers, and they feel good. It's a back-and-forth, shared process. Over a period of time you see students develop their competence and confidence, spread their wings, and together you wind up doing something that neither of you could have done by yourself. The whole is bigger than the sum of its parts. And, of course, the effect is magnified even more when you set out to do something that sensible people in the field say is just not possible. And then you do it!

I may be kidding myself, but sometimes I imagine that I see a physical reaction in students. They sort of rock back as if, *bam,* you just speared them like Cupid and they are forever changed. So you have a feeling you're doing something that endures; it's not an ephemeral thing. By working with students, you're literally planting seeds for the next generation. I tell my graduate students when we're writing scientific papers that we're really writing love letters to posterity. And I believe it. Maybe someone later on will read this paper and say, "Wow, yeah. What those guys did was primitive, but I can put it together with my work and we can go ahead." I've had that experience over and over.

The idea that science is highly competitive is actually misleading, because by nature it has to be primarily cooperative, and I like that a lot. Maybe in some of the glamorous biomedical fields there

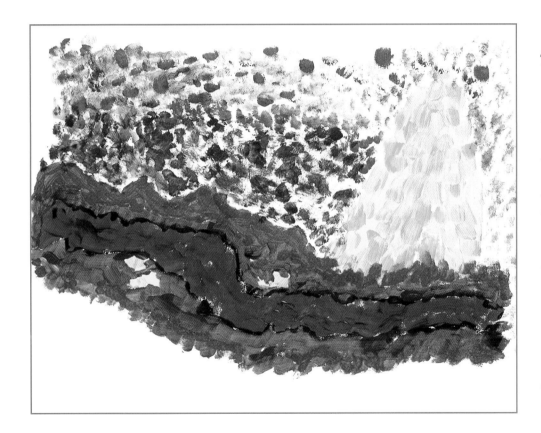

You know, painting is not so different than
doing science—you do something and only
later does it become clear that it has a logic of
its own. I recognize in this picture a memory
of the walk my wife and I did across England,
though I didn't have that in mind when I
started. When I started, I wanted something
that expressed, maybe, foolish optimism, but
also a sense of going up a mountain. I
wanted the mountain to offer the real satisfaction of enlarging your view of the world. And
the mountain is glowing yellow and orange,
which is warm and encouraging, like the sun.
Then I wanted a river flowing through. I'm
very aware of life going on from one generation to another. It's too narrow to just think
of your own life, rather than being part of a
continuum. I'm very aware of having this
precious legacy from my predecessors that I
want to enhance and pass on.

are hot and nasty races on occasion. But that's not at all typical. I guess I've always worked in what people call the lunatic fringe. As soon as a lot of people are working in a research area, I move out. I always feel I should be trying to do things other people aren't.

Maybe that relates to my love of open spaces. I find it tremendously satisfying to just walk and see a huge expanse of space. I like to say that my spirit expands to fill the space available, like a gas. I thrive in places that have lots of interesting people but where I can also go off by myself to think and write and have contact with trees and animals and rivers and mountains. Actually, that's some approximation of what I've been fortunate enough to enjoy for most of my life, so I guess it's not surprising that I think it's ideal.

I would love to see some of the limitations on people's lives lifted. Education is the most powerful thing. We squander so much in the way of human resources. I'm very worried about the environmental future of our planet, and the growth of world population is the biggest single factor in that. Most projections suggest it's going to level off close to eleven or twelve billion, roughly twice what we have now. Pollution's going to go up at least in proportion, especially if the developing world actually develops, though a lot of it isn't going to because of population growth. It breaks my heart to think of what we still spend on military things, and how much good that money could do elsewhere.

Again, education is the key. There's some hope that we can do markedly better than we have been with the use of worldwide TV and the Web. Those really are powerful things. My hope is that if enough people around the world come to think of themselves as global citizens, it may generate enough political pressure to increase the number of people who live truly fulfilling lives. It's heartbreaking to think what a small fraction of humanity even has any chance of that now.

I would also like to have more people recognize that there's something greater than mankind. I call it Mindkind, in which we recognize our kinship with the other marvelous creatures we share this planet with. For example, if we were to actually learn to speak with dolphins, I'm convinced we humans would prove the weaker in that pair. I've studied a little of the research, and we know that (a) dolphins are very intelligent; (b) they have their own language; (c) we don't yet understand it; (d) they understand ours better than we understand theirs. If we learned to understand their language, wouldn't that have an enormous impact on the way human beings think about our place in the universe?

I'd also be very surprised if in another fifty years we didn't know how to change one species into another, genetically. It won't be a practical, widespread thing. The National Football League is not going to be doing this because it wants to make linemen out of chimpanzees. But in terms of people's thinking, it will be very big, very important. Through history we've been faced with one piece of evidence after another showing us that we humans don't hold the highly exalted place in the universe that we like to think we have. And that's not a bad lesson for us to learn.   *November 24, 1997*

Richard HOLBROOKE

Permanent U.S. Representative to the United Nations (1999–2001); Chief Negotiator, Bosnian Peace Accords, Dayton (1995); Assistant Secretary of State for European and Canadian Affairs (1994–99)

Richard Holbrooke served as Permanent U.S. Representative to the UN from 1999 to 2001. In his previous position as assistant secretary of state for European and Canadian affairs, he was chief negotiator of the historic 1995 Dayton Peace Accords that ended the Bosnian war. Before those events Holbrooke served variously as U.S. ambassador to Germany, vice chairman of the investment bank Credit Suisse First Boston, managing director of Lehman Brothers investment bank, director of the Peace Corps, and managing editor of the quarterly *Foreign Policy Journal*. He also served as assistant secretary of state for East Asia and Pacific affairs from 1977 to 1981, a period marked by the establishment of full diplomatic relations with China.

The two problems that are most pernicious in the world today are racism in all its forms (including so-called ethnic conflict, which is just a euphemism for racism), which leads to, among other things, terrorism and fanaticism. And AIDS. I would hope for a world that has moved beyond its current wars and conflicts among peoples with ethnic and racial differences. And I would hope for a world in which the effort to prevent the spread of AIDS will finally have taken root. At the rate we're going, we're headed for over a hundred million people who will be HIV-positive, and who will eventually die of the disease or its complications. So those top two problems in turn jeopardize all the other great acts of progress in other areas.

When we first started talking about AIDS as more than a health problem, I thought I was simply asserting the obvious. AIDS is the worst health crisis in over six hundred years. But it's also much more because of the way it spreads, because of the fact that over 95 percent of the people who are HIV-positive don't know it, which means they're unintentional carriers, and because of the stigma attached to it. Because of all those things, it poses a greater threat to the economic, social, and political structure of societies than any other disease. And that makes it more than a health problem; it's a security problem as well.

Now, when we decided to use the occasion of America having the presidency of the UN Security Council, which by rotation came in January 2000, to devote the very first meeting of the new

85

This is very tough. I'm no good at this, but I like fiddling with the paints. I can see why people like to be painters. This looks like a very late de Kooning. You can call this "Holbrooke in his late de Kooning period, after de Kooning had Alzheimer's."

Now that's kind of an interesting color. I can see the therapeutic value of painting for high-strung people. What I'm thinking about here is just how late I am for the next meeting. Listen, Debra, this may be your moment, but it's my life. I'm being a good sport about this. What does the white look like? Oh! It's ruined; I ruined it! No, it's all right. I'll just convert it into something salvageable. I think the messy brush thing is good. We'll let people think this is a tree, so you can say that he did a slightly representational tree thing. That's it! That's it! Okay, Debra. This was fun.

millennium to a health issue, it developed that no one had done this before. There had been over four thousand Security Council meetings since 1945, and not one had been on a health issue. I didn't know that, and when we asserted that AIDS was a security issue, we were attacked by many traditional national security types.

But now, just barely a year later, there's no more debate. Everybody accepts the fact that it's a security issue. Now that hasn't saved lives directly, but it's changed the nature of the debate. Words have meaning, and now "national security" is not just about arms control and missiles; it's about threats to civilization. Here is a health issue that crosses international borders, jeopardizes political stability, and threatens societies. Some African countries, like Botswana, South Africa, Namibia, and Mozambique, are otherwise ready to emerge into an economic takeoff. But if a company has to hire two workers for every job because one is going to be HIV-positive . . . If millions of children are born carrying the disease and their mothers are dying, so that they are effectively orphans, whole societies will crumble. So we have a very, very serious situation.

Now, when you think of creating a world that's more perfect, that doesn't have this disease, you think first about the money involved. The UN secretary-general, Kofi Annan, who has been a great leader on this issue, was talking about a trust fund of $7 to $10 billion. That's a lot of money, but it will disappear into a bottomless pit unless it's backed up by a leadership effort from governments, and religious, business, and social leaders, to destigmatize

and educate the people. Education was the primary reason the growth of the disease was arrested in the United States. And even here, as recently as fifteen years ago, a lot of people thought you could get HIV from eating in the same restaurant as a gay waiter or something totally absurd. I remember New Yorkers who wouldn't get into a taxicab if the driver was Haitian. That was the level of ignorance we had here.

Now, Ted Turner and Bill Gates and George Soros, men who do have a lot of money, are using it in very valuable ways. At the end of 2000, when the UN was facing a crisis, Ted Turner offered us $31 million (a lot of money for an individual but not a huge amount of money against budgets) if that $31 million could be used to solve the UN budgetary crisis. And it was. It was creative philanthropy of the highest order.

Another example is Bill Gates's enlightened emphasis on putting money into research for vaccinations and vaccines for the diseases of poor countries, because the big pharmaceutical companies, as has been said, would rather find a cure for baldness than a cure for malaria, because they'll make more money. They'd rather develop Viagra than a cure for tuberculosis or a vaccine for TB. Gates cut through all this by putting up hundreds of millions of dollars of his own money for the vaccines in poorer countries.

Still, I do not share the view that this is the primary responsibility of private individuals and volunteerism. I think government leadership is required in these areas. And I think the United States, at the apogee of its wealth and power (no country in the world has ever been as rich or as powerful) should be able to figure out how to use money wisely, where it belongs.

Personally, I like challenges. I like to take on the toughest issues, and I'm willing to risk failure to do it. You know, if people in the public arena don't work on the most important issues of the day, if they just play it safe, why did they bother? Public service doesn't pay very much. So the only reason to do it is to help other people deal with the biggest problems of the day. I asked to be the negotiator for ending the war in Bosnia because I thought it was the toughest problem in the world, and one that I could make a contribution in. And as it turned out I *was* able to play a role in ending that war.

July 11, 2001

Patricia IRELAND

President, National Organization for Women
(1991–2001)

Patricia Ireland served as president of the National Organization for Women (NOW), the largest women's rights organization in the United States, for ten years, stepping down in August 2001. Before that she was a partner in a major Miami law firm and prior to that served as a flight attendant for Pan Am World Airlines.

The relationship between women and men is one of the first hierarchies of power that we learn when we're born into families. That's why I feel so strongly about the question of whether men have to be the leaders of families or whether women and men can stand as equal partners. It's a question of how children are raised, and how issues of violence get transmitted from generation to generation, or from family violence to violence in the culture. I really see the improvement of women's lives as being key to improving the life of any community, or the general well-being of a country or culture.

There are still places in the world where the types of discrimination are so egregious, like the historic practice of female genital mutilation, affecting millions of women. Of course, it's easier to see problems in somebody else's culture. And I wouldn't necessarily want to direct attention away from what goes on in the United States, because the violence against women in our homes here is often brutal and debilitating, and it still keeps women from participating fully in the life of this country.

When I think of my hopes for the world, I think first of really addressing the root causes of violence. Family violence in our own homes is overwhelmingly directed toward females, though violence against children is sometimes perpetuated by women. And hate crimes—the playing out of our politics in violence—whether it's government violence, or the folks who now claim justifiable homicide, killing doctors and abortion-rights supporters, or violence against lesbians and gays for

89

their sexual orientation. I come at most of these problems from the perspective of improving women's lives and empowering women.

I would also like to see a world in which we have reversed the wage and wealth gap. The issues that get most visibility are often literally sexy: sexual harassment, abortion rights, or sexual orientation. I worry sometimes that we overlook the economic issues. People say, "Oh, economic issues are so complex. I don't even know who the villain is." If we call for a march on abortion rights, or on violence against women, we can fill the streets. But if we call for a march on economic justice, we get a very low response. Maybe people think the problem is too big.

What I really want, and it's something that's already started, is the full integration of women into the social, political, economic, and legal aspects of the culture. Many people think we've made such incredible progress toward that end, and we have. And yet the U.S. Senate is still 91 percent male; 95 to 97 percent of the top CEOs, or even just top management, of the largest corporations are men.

I was quite taken at the Beijing Conference on Women with finding that the Vatican had felt compelled to send women to speak on their behalf. And even that part of the world that is so funda-

mentalist that they don't want women to even have a voice had sent women to the conference to argue, "No, we don't want to participate in sports where men can see our bodies. We want to stay in a more secluded environment. It's our choice." I, of course, disagree vigorously with their position, but it did catch my eye that even the most conservative forces in the world felt that women had been empowered enough to speak on their own behalf.

The point is that women just have different life experiences and bring a different set of priorities to the table. That's a gross generalization, of course, subject to the same flaws as any gross generalization. I know there are good men that we work with on these issues and there are women I have nothing in common with politically. Sometimes we kick open the door and someone we disagree with walks through.

I have less interest in men understanding women better, or being more sensitive, than I do in equality and fairness. And if that fairness comes because people have understanding, then great. If it comes because it's required by the culture and they at first don't understand but do comply, I might settle for that. It's a start.

October 20, 1997

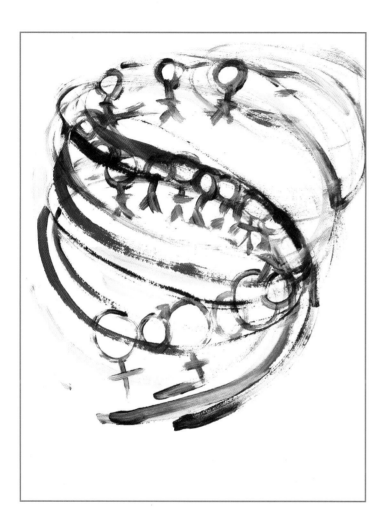

Some of us just don't have our creativity in our visual imagery. I can't think of anything more difficult to do. This is just a swirl of colors and stick figures, some men and women, representing an optimistic view of moving forward and upward, not without a lot of tumult, not without a lot of chaos. I'm envisioning this swirl of ideas and impulses that may go around but that is a general forward spiral of progress on the issues I care about. It might mean looking beyond the things that historically have divided us by sex. It's about continually transcending who we used to be, moving from, say, bearbaiting to Monday Night Football. *I see that as some progress, even if it's not where I'd like us to end up.*

Knight KIPLINGER

Editor in Chief, Kiplinger's Personal Finance Magazine; *Editor,* The Kiplinger Letter

Knight Kiplinger is editor of *The Kiplinger Letter,* the nation's leading business-forecasting publication, and editor in chief of *Kiplinger's Personal Finance Magazine.* He has covered business, economic, and political trends for nearly three decades as a newspaper reporter, Washington bureau chief, and editor. He is also the author of several books, including *World Boom Ahead* (1998), and is a frequent guest on major television and radio programs.

92

The most challenging job I face each day is as a father and a husband, and everything else is secondary. I have three teenagers, and rearing them to be well-adjusted, productive young adults is the hardest job I've ever faced. If we do it reasonably well, it should give us much more satisfaction than any professional success, but we'll never know until many years later. Children are works in progress. As a society, we don't pay enough attention to our children. We're overindulgent materially and underindulgent emotionally and spiritually.

In my ideal world all children would be reared at home by one of their parents, mother or father, until about the age of four. Children would not be put in day care at six months so that Father and Mother can continue their careers unimpeded by the inconvenience of parenthood. (I underscore the fact that this is not solely a mother's responsibility.) But many of the social problems we face in America today relate to the inadequate supervision of young children.

For the larger world, I want the winds of self-determination and self-governance, which have been blowing very strongly for the last ten or fifteen years, to spread over the entire globe so that everybody on Earth lives in a democratic political and social system. The largest groups of people without self-determination are in China and the Arab Middle East, where democracy is virtually nonexistent. And of course there are smaller nations, such as North Korea and Cuba, living under very repressive communism. In China, you have an authoritarian system, which will probably gradually

This painting is about crosscurrents: flows of trade, capital, people, ideas, and technology throughout the globe. It's multidirectional; it's free and uncontrollable by governments. It's self-interested, determined by people's needs, wants, and desires. It's also somewhat chaotic. So you have the dispersal of science and technology worldwide, the democratization of ideas, and if it looks messy and untidy, that's kind of the idea. Besides the fact that I am not an artist and it would look messy and untidy anyway. (Now you can see why I went into journalism.)

yield to self-determination through the mechanism of free markets.

So my second great wish for the world is that free economic markets continue their ascent. And those two are preconditions for my greatest wish, which is that personal incomes and living standards will rise dramatically in today's less developed nations.

The history of humankind has been one of gradual improvement in the material well-being of people: greater longevity, improving diet, and a rising material living standard, by which I mean the creature comforts of life. The ability to live with reasonable certainty that you will not starve or die of an infectious disease at an early age. Happiness, though, is not quantifiable, so it's hard to crank into that equation.

Some indices of social, emotional, or spiritual health go in the opposite direction of measurements for material living standards. If I envision a better world in which the mother or father stays home with the children until the age of four, that's income forgone. That means the family would show a lower "standard of living" if we define that by household expenditure or consumption. But the spiritual and emotional standard of living in that family may go up.

Another thing I wish for in the next century is the ascent of women worldwide. We forget how unusual equal educational opportunity, equal access to credit or business opportunity, is in the world. Only very recently in some African nations have little girls had the same opportunity to public education that boys have had. Only recently in India, Pakistan, and Bangladesh have women had

access to microcredit to start small businesses. The ascent of women is obviously good for women, but it's also critical for societies. Women already do well over half of all the work performed in the world today. They make and process food; they process fiber into clothing; they do household work. Most of this is off the books today. But I believe the surge of women into market economies will be a big factor in strengthening economic growth and raising living standards worldwide. So it's one thing I wish for.

My perfect world is also a world in which families have as many children as they are able to support financially. In the advanced world that would mean larger families and in less advanced countries it would mean smaller families. It's regrettable that the spirit of zero population growth has taken hold to such a degree in the advanced nations that we see declining populations over the next two decades in Europe and Japan. The United States is right to allow a high level of immigration.

I also wish for the obliteration of race as a descriptive classifier of human beings. Today, we classify people by race for the stated, intended purpose of assisting them, when in fact it just undermines the concept of judging people by their individual merit. I support voluntary affirmative action by people who wish to show some modest tilt toward a certain group, but governmental quotas and targets are antithetical to human progress. So I wish for a society with a greater emphasis on individual responsibility, individual worth, and individual merit in all things. *January 22, 1999*

Richard KLAUSNER

Senior Fellow and Special Adviser on Counterterrorism to the Presidents, National Academies (since 2002); Director, National Cancer Institute (1995–2001)

Richard Klausner, M.D., became senior fellow and special adviser on counterterrorism to the presidents of the National Academies in 2002, acting as a liaison between academy scientists and the White House Office of Science and Technology Policy. He served for six years, beginning in 1995, as director of the National Cancer Institute (NCI), where he was widely recognized as a passionate and effective spokesman for the nation's war on cancer.

A large number of simple organisms—bacteria, for instance—are particularly interesting and spectacularly successful precisely because they are very adaptable and can thrive in multiple environments. And we humans are particularly good at that, too. I think, emotionally, not only are we good at it, but we need it. We need our environment to be varied and varying, or we get bored. There's an interesting book, called *Anatomy of Restlessness,* by an author I like very much, Bruce Chatwin. He says the nature of man is to be a nomad, and he talks about how important it is to be in changing environments. So I actually would like to see a varied environment that provides lots of interest and change. The thing that's most difficult is an environment that's static, and that's how we think of prisons. Prison is the absolute definition of constancy, coupled with bareness, but I think it's the constancy that's most difficult.

In the area I spend my time thinking about, medicine and health, I certainly hope that our ability to understand disease has progressed enough so that we can dramatically reduce the burden of disease. That's easy to say, though there really is no such thing as a world without disease; it's just not biologically possible. That's part of a broader hope I have, which is that the ethos and ethics of science at its best is more permanent in the world than it is. I think that we are extraordinarily scientifically illiterate. And I don't mean that we just don't know facts about science. There is a way of thinking, which is being open to asking questions. Science is extraordinarily democratic, in that it

95

respects the power of evidence and not the power of authority. So I would hope that the world has learned to be more scientifically literate. We're so far from that now. We have so much trouble dealing with contradictions among intuition, bias, belief, our openness to evidence, and our willingness to accept preconceived notions without asking whether they make sense. I think it gets us into a lot of trouble and creates issues like racism and tribalism.

I think man has always been confronted with enormous ethical problems: Do you kill your neighbor? How do you set up a legal system? What are loyalties? How do you help people? How do you not help people? And there are new ways to frame ethical dilemmas that emerge with technologies. I am not an ethicist, but I am not convinced that we are creating fundamentally new ethical dilemmas about respect for life, freedom, and individuality as we create new technologies. Is the ethics of killing a small number of people with immature technology fundamentally different than the ethics of killing a larger number of people as our technology "advances"? Is our technology running ahead of our ethics? I'm not sure that's the right picture. I think the real issue is, Are we constantly struggling with the fact that almost all aspects of human endeavor, discovery, politics, have enormous ethical consequences?

Technical questions are easier than ethical questions and always have been. I think the novelistic impact of what science and technology does in some way pushes us to deal with ethical issues that have always been there. But the technologies are so dramatic, they so cap-

ture our imagination, that they focus us to have ethical discussions. So, in a paradoxical way, the creation of the atom bomb created a discussion of ethical responsibilities to the planet that we always needed to have. But the technology focused it. I think the same thing is happening with biologic challenges. They're so stimulating to our imagination, running both to the dark and to the optimistic, that they remind us of our need to cope with ethical issues.

I'm not convinced of this axiom that whatever technology we're capable of, we'll use. It's remarkable how often technology is just forgotten, lost, ignored, replaced with other things. I'm certainly not frightened of the dark side of what technology will allow us to do. It's unclear to me why we have to assume that, because in our worst imagination we can fantasize misusing something, that we're going to do that. The dynamics of the application, use, and threat of technology is very complex. It doesn't follow a simple rule like, Whatever we can do, we'll do.

The mysteries of cancer are at the center of the most fundamental mysteries of life itself, and that's really exciting. Cancer has been basically a prerational disease; we've known very little about it. And until now our approach to it has been through empiricism rather than through science. What I want to be part of is the fundamental transformation of our approach to this most complex of human diseases from guesswork and empiricism to design. Cancer is a disease of altered gene expression. There is a fraction of the time when there are definable, inherited predispositions to cancer.

Well, I must say, I have no idea what image I want, but I'm very attracted to these colors. . . . I guess I'm thinking here about a scene I remembered on the island of Ocracoke, off the coast of North Carolina. My wife and I were there with friends, and we all had little kids. We were sitting on a dune looking out across the beach, and our three little kids were running and playing and looking very puppy-like. And we all sat and stared and recognized how fleeting this was going to be. At least that's what I was thinking about. That's what this image reminds me of.

But cancer is actually a process of genetic change, and of course you don't inherit genetic change, you experience it. It's a process in which cells change their behavior because some patterns in the sixty to one hundred thousand instructions that determine the behavior of a cell are gradually altered.

Ultimately, we will understand each cancer in terms of being able to read and interpret the molecular fingerprint that's a part of it. We'll no longer be diagnosing things simply as prostate cancer, or breast cancer, because that's only how the disease behaves. We'll actually be able to let the cells tell us, This is what I am; this is how to treat me; this is what will happen, how quickly I will grow. That's going to happen. Prostate cancer or breast cancer will be defined not by what we have been doing for a hundred years, which is looking at it under a microscope. That's sort of like looking at a person and saying, "I know what you look like, therefore I know how you're going to behave." It doesn't work very well. That's what we've been doing with cancer. What we want to do is get inside and read the blueprint of each cancer. Then we'll know what works. It's very exciting. It *is* going to happen.

I think we do have, I must say, a remarkable experiment in the United States, with all our terrible problems with racial and economic inequality, of attempting to come to grips with the idea of diversity and a kind of antitribalism. But fanaticism is very frightening. I don't know whether there's more or less of it now than there's always been. But watching it unfold all over is really worrisome. What's worrisome is that I don't see it going away. I don't know why I'd expect it to, but that's the hope each generation has for the next.

February 27, 1997

William KRISTOL

Founder, Publisher, and Editor, The Weekly Standard (*since 1995*)

I very much hope for an America in which families are stronger, where a third of kids aren't born out of wedlock. I also hope that the culture becomes healthier and that everyone doesn't grow up being ironic about everything. I don't know if I'd want the opposite of irony, but it would be nice to have something between postmodern irony and Victorian earnestness.

Another thing I very much hope for is that we don't go down the road that it would seem we are, which is to a brave new world of cloning, and a science that just runs over all ethical limits. I would describe the threat as a combination of scientific rationalism with value relativism, a "who's-to-say-what's-right-for-anyone?" attitude. We now have a society that's lost the notion that there are objective rights and wrongs. And, on the other hand, we have all this scientific progress. I think the two together are quite dangerous. Who's to say that we shouldn't create embryos for the sake of destroying them? Our generation grew up fearing *1984*. I think the greater threat now is a brave new world, not the kind of political totalitarianism described in *1984*, which Huxley actually said to Orwell in a letter written in 1948 or '49.

I think you can have good trends and bad trends going on at the same time, so it's too simplistic to say it's all getting worse, or all getting better. But I guess I would say I'm mildly pessimistic, in general. I think the world frustrates most good plans. I also think it's going to be very hard to stop some of the impulses of modern times that are damaging people's lives. My father once described

Do I have to draw? I think I'll pass on this because (a) I'm not imaginative visually, and (b) the things I care about are not particularly visual things. I'm such a bad drawer that I'd be embarrassed to do it. Okay, I'll do my best.

I'll try to draw a book, but you're going to have to explain it's a book because I can't draw. So much of what I've done has come from books. It's the way I think. The friends I've kept over the years are people with whom I can have a good argument and a serious intellectual exchange. Thinking things through is in a way the highest human activity. So that's my perfect world.

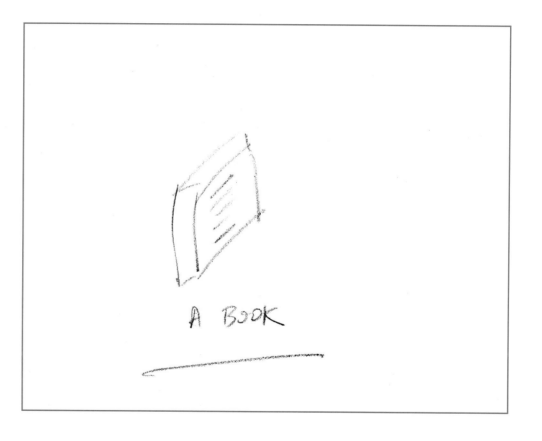

A BOOK

himself as a cheerful pessimist, and I guess I'd sign on to that. It's pretty hard to improve things in the world.

On the other hand, I think recently there has been a healthy willingness to look back at older thinkers and at religions and wonder if there isn't some truth there that we've neglected. So in that respect I would argue that young people today maybe have greater hope than a lot of young people did fifty years ago, who were just told they could ignore all that old stuff.

Whether it will all pan out as something serious or worthwhile, I don't know. It's a funny time. The level of political debate has certainly gone down in the last forty, fifty, sixty years. Today, everything is emotions and kind of silly. But there's also this countertrend of greater intellectual depth. So I'm hopeful.

I've been involved with a couple of philanthropies over the years, and it's not easy to give money away intelligently. But if I had money to give away right now, the cause I'd probably choose is Jewish education. I'm concerned about Jewish continuity in the United States. For all the wealth in the American Jewish community, so much of their money goes to everything except Jewish things.

July 19, 2001

Paul KRUGMAN

Professor of Economics, Princeton University;
Columnist, The New York Times
(since 1999)

Paul Krugman has been a regular columnist for *The New York Times* since 1999. He is also professor of economics at Princeton University. During the Reagan administration, in 1982 and '83, Krugman served as chief staffer at the Council of Economic Advisers. He is a founder of the "new theory" on international trade, an expert on international finance, and the author of several books, including *The Age of Diminished Expectations* (1997), which quickly became a cult classic in economics. In 1991 Krugman received the coveted John Bates Clark Medal from the American Economic Association.

Every three or four weeks I make a mammoth effort to bring this office slightly under control, and then it quickly deteriorates again. I spend most of my life in an extremely messy office with piles of stuff and constant pressure. I mostly enjoy that, but I need escapes. So my wife and I take a relatively large number of vacations, typically someplace warm and sunny. But if I spent all my time in beautiful places, I'd get bored.

I have an image of an ideal society. I'd like the world to look like the impression I had of Sweden in the summer of 1982. Stockholm in the summer is extremely pleasant, but the thing that really got me was that no one was hungry, no one was poor, and there was no crime to speak of. It was this relatively egalitarian, prosperous, cheerful society with no real extreme suffering, and no class animosities. Everybody seemed to have a little house in the country and a boat. So, prosperity, relative equality, a well-cared-for city, museums in good shape, parks well maintained. The fact is that even Sweden doesn't look like that anymore, but that's what I'd like to see.

We hardly ever talk about it, but the worst thing about today's world is that there is actually a fourth world, countries where there is no hope at all, nothing is moving forward, and where no one is participating in economic progress. It's almost all of sub-Saharan Africa, parts of South America, parts of Asia, close to a billion people when you put it all together. I would like to imagine a world that doesn't have a fourth world. It's probably too much to hope that there won't be some extremely

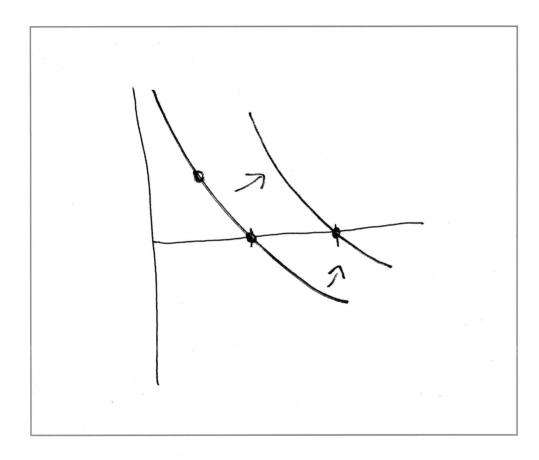

Oh, God! I'm literally incapable of drawing a straight line! I'm not sure I can do this! I'm so sorry; I'm basically a black-and-white kind of guy. I tend to think in terms of schematics, though of course those don't exactly have an emotional content. I am a big believer in the power and usefulness of diagrams.

I just spent the last couple weeks trying to set straight what I think about Japan, and I came up with a diagram that makes me happy, because it explains how you can get into the trap they're in. But it's not a happy diagram. Actually, it's more like a picture of unhappiness. I don't have a picture of happiness. This diagram is about the choices they have. This diagram says that everybody is looking at this problem the wrong way, and that there is possibility out there. It doesn't include the best-case scenario, but it's my best effort to save the world.

poor countries, but I would hope for a world in which there are no big stretches on the map where you could say, "Economic progress doesn't happen here."

I'd also like to see a world where international interventions would really prevent things like Rwanda. You know, something like that doesn't happen in Europe because if French-speaking and Flemish-speaking Belgians were to start shooting each other, their neighbors would keep it from going beyond that, right? I want a world where that's true not just in Western Europe or North America but everywhere.

I've seen a lot of abuse of money in politics, really bad ideas getting promoted because they happen to appeal to wealthy people. And that has given legitimacy to some bad, in some cases almost evil, ideas. What I have in mind is the right-wing think tank network. Look at the amount of damage the Coors family has done by funding the Heritage Foundation, or the Koch brothers have done by funding the Cato Institute. If I had a lot of money, I would give it to something specifically dedicated to people who say things that offend orthodoxies on both sides.

I'm a solitary worker. For the most part I sit with a pad of paper on my lap staring into space or at a computer screen. My best moments are when I figure something out about the world that I didn't understand before, or when I find a way to say something that I hadn't found before. When something like that goes right, I'll spend a couple of days feeling very excited, and that feeling is probably the single thing that drives me most.

I find I get more cynical as I get older, though. It's just that things that are exciting the first time you do them become less so, obviously. So many things, like being asked for advice by important people or publishing in very visible places, were a thrill the first time, but become just, All right, done that. What's the old line? "Ye little know with how little wisdom the world is governed"? Once you actually see what goes on, you're a lot less impressed with it, and it's much less fun to be part of it. Even the joy of figuring something out is less intense after the fifteenth time. It seems that I've arrived, and having arrived is a lot less fun than traveling.

May 11, 1998

Delano LEWIS

U.S. Ambassador to South Africa (1999–2001); President and CEO, National Public Radio (1994–98); Cochair, National Information Infrastructure Advisory Council (1994–96)

Delano Lewis served as U.S. ambassador to the Republic of South Africa for two years, beginning in 1999. He was president and CEO of National Public Radio, the nation's largest public broadcasting network, from 1994 to 1998. He also served on the board of directors for Black Entertainment Television and as cochair of the National Information Infrastructure Advisory Council, which provided policy recommendations to the Clinton administration on how best to develop America's communication network.

If I could wave a magic wand, I'd give everybody a job. In this country it means so much. I grew up as an only child in Kansas with a father who spent thirty-seven years working on the Santa Fe Railroad. This guy with a grade-school education would get up every day, put on his uniform, his shoes shined, and he was very proud of what he did. His paycheck meant something; it certainly meant something to us. And he didn't want to retire. There's something about being able to produce. Also, I don't get hung up on Ph.D.s and master's degrees. I really think of education as skills training, learning how to do something productive.

I started out as a Peace Corps staff person in Nigeria and Uganda, and I still believe that, if you're going to make a difference in this society and around the world, you need to train local community and indigenous leaders. If you can train people to take charge of their own lives, they'll make the difference, because they're the ones who know their community; they understand what's important.

The problem with USAID, our foreign aid projects, is that we take our American know-how and our American culture and say, "Here's what we think you should do." And we make some terrible blunders. We're constantly shortchanging the locals.

So the main thing about a perfect world is that we need to know more about one another. The world is much too divided, country to country, right now. There's still too much racial, ethnic, and

105

*I envision the ideal world as a circle, much
more of a holistic thing than it is right now.
But that will be my ideal. I also feel that
there are a lot of overlapping cultures, and
overlapping entities, in this ideal world, and
where they intersect they have some collegiality.
Also, I want this image to say that we need a
shared vision for this new world in order for
things to happen. So this ideal world is various peoples and cultures working together,
sharing a vision for the future, and making
some progress for the benefit of the greatest
good. This image conveys a sense of purpose
for me.*

106

religious animosity, based on ignorance. I would like to see those things diminished, but I would add that charity begins at home, and there's so much to do here in the United States even as we try to influence the rest of the world.

I know that if technology keeps booming as it has been, it'll have a tremendous impact on what this country looks like, what kinds of jobs we get, and what kind of society we live in. But the thing that will impact this country most is people who get in, organize, and make a difference. That really matters. I mean, we wouldn't be out of Vietnam if people hadn't organized to say, Stop. We wouldn't have had advances in civil rights if no one stood up and said, This is the way it should be. So leadership is extremely important.

I also feel very strongly about the plight of the African-American male, and that's not a sexist concern, it's just one I happen to have because I am an African-American male, and I have four sons. I can identify with those who struggle with the legacy of slavery, the breakdown of families and communities, the economics of those communities, or the lack of cohesion. My view is that a lot of African-American males have been pushed out so that they feel trapped, and they're nonproductive. If you go to the jails of this country, they're filled with all kinds of minorities, for the most part African-Americans and Hispanics. They can produce children but hardly anything else, and it's very, very sad. They've dropped out of school; they don't have skills; they can't produce; and their self-images are very poor. I worry about that a lot.   *July 16, 1997*

Jessica MATHEWS

President, Carnegie Endowment for International Peace (since 1997)

Jessica Mathews was appointed president of the Carnegie Endowment for International Peace in 1997, after having served as director of the Washington program for the Council on Foreign Relations. Before this, Mathews had been founding vice president and director of research at the World Resources Institute. In the late 1970s she was director of the Office of Global Issues of the National Security Council, and in 1993 she returned to government as deputy to the undersecretary of state for global affairs. She served on the editorial board of *The Washington Post* from 1980 to 1982, later writing a weekly column for *The Post*, which appeared in newspapers nationwide and in *The International Herald Tribune*.

108

I hope population will pretty much stabilize. And I hope that mankind will learn to live on this planet with a much lighter environmental footprint, able to extract as much quality of life as we do now, but with a much lighter impact on the planet. I also hope for much less poverty and extreme inequity between rich and poor.

If I had a lot of extra money to give away, I guess I'd give it for environmental work, partly because I know that field could absorb it usefully. The core issues are climate and biodiversity habitat preservation, open space preservation, and the management of the basic resource systems of land, forest, water, and fisheries. You may say there's been tremendous progress in the environmental area in the last ten years, and yet most of the systems you look at and measure are getting worse rather than better. But if you think a little bit longer term, you can see fifteen things we know we could do. I guess I'm optimistic that eventually they will get done.

In international affairs there's a radical, almost revolutionary, shift in the center of gravity from a world completely dominated by states to one in which nonstate actors like businesses, NGOs, and international organizations play a major role. It's probably too soon to tell what the implications will be. That'll depend on whether the private sector begins to take account of its broader policy role, and recognize its wider accountability.

The state's role is more and more going to be just to set the rules by which the other actors

Let me describe this because I can't draw. These are the elements of a perfect world: challenge, people (but not too many people, not too crowded), peace. I have no visual association with peace; to me it's just the absence of conflict. Also something beautiful and challenging, which is this mountain, a hard thing. Those are the elements of a perfect world, except that this picture doesn't have enough nature in it. That would be the other element—abundance, living things. If I could draw a great jungle, I would.

operate. For instance, governments have to make rules so that what are now externalities in the market become priced, and therefore become part of what the market will produce. Right now the market doesn't worry about producing jobs. It worries about producing income and profits, but not jobs. Well, that could be changed. It doesn't worry about whether or not it produces pollution, because pollution has not been priced. But that can be changed. If the rules change, the market will produce a different set of outcomes.

But it's not clear yet whether that will happen. If the state backs away, as it has recently, and leaves almost every decision to business, there are an awful lot of things that business can and will do to improve its own bottom line that will be very bad for other interests. So, it's too soon to tell.

I also think the information revolution is changing everything. These technologies empower the individual immensely vis-à-vis the state. They basically erase the impact of geographic distance, and they're neutral as regards national boundaries, so they could make it impossible to tax transactions the way we do now.

They also make it possible to move everything crucial to the economic sphere—capital, resources, ideas, and information, everything except people—instantaneously. The one fixed entity is people, and I think that situation is going to create a tremendous tension that will require readjustment.

These new communications technologies are globalizing technologies, obviously, but they're also fragmenting technologies.

They're creating millions of tiny niches. And whether their net effect will be principally to globalize or principally to fragment, we don't know yet. But they'll change what it means to live in a community.

There are a lot of things to read and think about and a lot of personal relationships that one doesn't have time for. My life has always been this tremendous tension between family, children, and career—wanting to live too many different lives at once.

My family owns a cabin on a hundred-acre farm in Virginia, and I think it's my favorite place in the world. It's very remote, completely quiet, with a view of the mountains. I need the outdoors. I often think I'd be happier if I just quit work and rode my horse and lived in a barn. But I also know that I never would be, so I never actually do that. That's because I also thrive in a high-energy environment, one where most of the work is intellectual as opposed to managerial. I know people in this field who've gotten sick to death of conferences, but I still find them very stimulating. So, intellectual discussion and input from others are part of my perfect world.

The syndicated newspaper column I wrote was an enormous burden, a huge effort, but also very rewarding. Every week there had to be something, and it had to be good. I had to get up at four in the morning, and I'd think, Why am I doing this? But I got more from that work than anything else I've ever done. I didn't fully appreciate it until I didn't have it anymore. Not just the writing, but the reading it took to do the writing. Looking back on it now, it was worth every minute. *February 10, 1998*

Derek McGINTY

Anchor, World News Now, ABC NEWS *(since 2001); Cohost,* Capitol Sunday; *Correspondent,* Real Sports, *HBO*

Derek McGinty was named anchor of *World News Now* (ABC NEWS) in 2001. He is also cohost of *Capitol Sunday* (WJLA in New York) and a correspondent for *Real Sports* (HBO). He worked previously as a correspondent for *Public Eye* with Bryant Gumbel on CBS. He also hosted the nationally broadcast *Straight Talk with Derek McGinty* (WETA) and the Emmy-nominated *Here and Now.* McGinty first became popular with his award-winning talk show *The Derek McGinty Show* on the public radio station WAMU in Washington, D.C.

I really hope that the world continues to evolve socially. We complain about where we are, but we spent a long time smacking each other in the head before we got to where we are today. It's incredible how far we've come in the last hundred years.

For example, at one point in the 1930s Franklin Roosevelt, a man in a wheelchair who could not walk, was the president of the United States. But he couldn't let the American people know he was a cripple, because he wouldn't be accepted as a leader. We've come a long way in our view of what's valuable in a human being. We've decided that you can still be valuable even if you can't walk. We've also decided as a society that race ought not to be a factor in the way we treat people. Have we reached that goal? No. But that's our goal; it's our ideal. And that's evolution.

What's acceptable and what's not acceptable? How do we treat children? Are there child-labor laws? To me all those things say that our society is trying to reach a point where we deal with each other more humanely.

The question is, Will a lack of resources drive us back? If things get bad, and we're all struggling, will our ability to evolve deteriorate? It's like *Lord of the Flies.* When things get bad, people get savage, and it throws that evolutionary process out of whack.

I would also like the world to be a place where we take long-range concerns about the environment seriously before they begin to have an impact. We're getting to the point where we can't just say, "Oh my God! It's about to happen. Now let's change." We've got to change a long time before things like global warming start impacting us directly. We're very bad at doing the painful thing that makes sense early. We're bad at not eating too much, not smoking too much, not drinking too much. We really need to focus on taking short-term pain for long-term gain. Of course, that's easy for me to say.

So far, most of my dreams have come true. I've been blessed with a good home, good parents, a job I like. I'm not rich, but I don't need much. If I can have enough money for a decent house and some nice toys to play with, and if I can send my kids to college (if I ever get married and have kids . . .), I don't need a lot. I have very few complaints.

I do have a faith that every time we come to the edge of dumbness, there will be some great change that will make us back away. And every time we do, we'll evolve a little more. We'll get a little more in tune with the things we need to do. That's the thing about humanity. We're the only creature that gets to build on what's happened before, because of our language and our ability to transmit from generation to generation. So I hope that will continue to happen.

I do worry about the fact that a lot of people are afraid to explore ideas that are out of the mainstream. If somebody expresses a thought that's not considered acceptable, they're shouted down. People say, "Oh, he should be fired from his job!" You don't have to agree with somebody, but let's first find out what the person meant, and then at least we could understand each other better. If their philosophy is faulty, you can poke holes in it.

I'm no aged sage, but the older I get, the more concerned I've gotten about what happens to young people. I've got two nephews and a niece, and I really am concerned about the kind of world they're going to have to live in. I really want them to have opportunities, places where they can succeed. I hope this remains a country where young people continue to grow up and find themselves.

April 1, 1997

The rocket delineates the fact that we're a high-tech planet; we've got technology and we can do stuff. But you will note that my planet is also very green and blue, so that we're also environmentally friendly. We handle ourselves environmentally as brilliantly as we handle ourselves technologically. That's my perfect world.

Ingrid NEWKIRK

President and Cofounder, People for the Ethical Treatment of Animals (since 1980)

Ingrid Newkirk became cofounder and president of People for the Ethical Treatment of Animals, the largest animal rights organization in the world, in 1980. She is the author of six books and numerous articles on the treatment of animals in homes, slaughterhouses, circuses, and laboratories. She coordinated the first arrest in U.S. history of a laboratory scientist on animal cruelty charges and led efforts to terminate the Department of Defense's "wound laboratory" animal tests and General Motors' crash tests using live animals. She served previously as a Maryland state law enforcement officer.

My perfect world personally would be nothing but writing and reading, but in my professional life I like to live with a sense of crisis. I don't have a laid-back attitude toward much of anything.

I'm particularly fond of the more decrepit parts of the New Jersey coastline. It was once vibrant and busy, but it's now overgrown with weeds, very depressed. In looking at that area, which has the additional benefit of being on the coast, it seems that there's enormous potential to do something about the animals who need to be looked after. In areas where people have little, you typically find animals who have nothing.

In riding through that area I once found a mixed German shepherd with her puppy dragging a long rope along a highway and in terrible shape, covered with oil, with their ribs showing. That's the sort of thing that just cries out for help in a generally affluent society where people haven't a clue about how the other side lives.

In Aspen, Colorado, there's potential, but since there isn't the economic depression, it doesn't fill me with the same thoughts and ideas about how to improve things.

It's not very practical, but my dream for the world is that eating animals will become a thing of the past. That we will soon look back and say, "Good Lord, do you know what we used to do?" It's repulsive and hideous—like slavery. If you watch *Star Trek*, everyone is vegan in space. Only if they

Cool! You want me to draw? But I haven't got an artistic bone in my body. It's very sad. How about cut and paste? I always thought if ever I retire I would love to make a mosaic of wonderful patterns. But that's not going to happen. Let's see what we've got here. Hopeless! Completely hopeless!

A perfect world would be something like the Christian Garden of Eden, where animals and people live in love and respect for all forms of life, no matter what package they come in. Animals would be free to enjoy themselves. It's first about enjoyment and the symbiotic relationship between giving love and getting love, respecting that people have their space and animals have their space, a very crude version of the Garden of Eden. I don't expect a perfect world. But I've grown to understand that even little things can have an enormous impact.

115

portray a really vulgar, barbaric society do they let those creatures eat other beings.

The second thing is that we have come shamefully slowly to stopping animal experimentation. We can't use orphans, or gypsies, or men in the military without their knowledge. You can't use homosexuals, or prisoners of war, so you shouldn't be able to use animals simply because you have the might to do so. Nowadays we have the whole human genome on the Web. We have high-tech methodology; things are getting faster and faster. Yet we still experiment on animals.

If I could, I'd like to turn the whole school system upside down. The emphasis now is on making money, categorizing things, labeling things, becoming clever, without learning how to get along with others, how to be decent, the Golden Rule, kindness, empathy, relationships. If you teach a child to be empathetic toward a caterpillar, you do as much for the child as you do for the caterpillar. That child will be able to look at somebody who doesn't appear to be like them in any way and empathize.

There's an excellent program called Share the World, which simply asks children to put themselves in the place of others. It has a number of scenarios, and the children move themselves around from one character to another asking, "What would you do? How would you feel?"

I grew up in India, and the Indian poet Tagore had disciples who toured rich little girls' schools like mine. When they came to my school, we were all stuck-up little snobs, with no sense of the neediness in the world. But the disciples talked to us about nature, beauty, simplicity, kindness, looking out for others. It took a long time to settle in, but eventually I think it helped me.

Reincarnation would be my worst nightmare. You can be a happy person, but unless you live in a dream—oblivious to what's happening to the elderly, children, animals, war—you can't really hope to come back into it again. It's a life of service, and extreme trouble. Human beings treat others, including their closest, in such god-awful ways.

December 1, 2000

Jim NICHOLSON

U.S. Ambassador to the Holy See (since 2001); Chairman, Republican National Committee (1997–2000)

Jim Nicholson was appointed U.S. ambassador to the Holy See (Vatican) in 2001. He was elected chairman of the Republican National Committee (RNC) in 1997, a year during which the Republican Party broke all records for fund-raising. His tenure as RNC chairman culminated in the historic Republican victories of the 2000 elections: winning the presidency, the Congress, and a majority of governorships and state legislatures. In 2000 Nicholson received the prestigious Horatio Alger Award, recognizing his impressive climb from humble beginnings.

My ideal world would be a world of free people having the basic necessities in life, particularly food and the fulfillment of a job. And it would be a world in which people do not suffer addictions that debilitate their lives, or the people around them.

My father suffered seriously from the disease of alcoholism. There were seven kids in our family and, because he was chronically ill, we were chronically poor. Often, food was an issue. We lived in a tenant farmhouse in rural Iowa after my father went broke farming after two crop failures in a row, then really became a very serious alcoholic. So, I was brought up in poverty and depravity, and things were often very dysfunctional.

My mother, though, was a rock. She used to tell us that in spite of all this if we kids worked hard, and studied hard, and prayed hard, we'd have a good life in this country. She had this enduring spirit and faith that sustained us all.

We did work hard, and we did get a decent education. I went to a one-room schoolhouse through the fifth grade, a two-room schoolhouse through the eighth grade, and then into town to high school. Having overcome these circumstances, we hung in there, my siblings and I. All seven of us have been to college, and five of us have postgraduate degrees. I think in this country that if you set some goals and work hard, then just about anything is possible. I also have strong faith in God, and I pray regularly, which I think helps. I was lucky enough to get admitted to West Point. When

In this painting I've put a little school, which represents education. And over here a church, which is very important to me. And here is a cemetery, the gravestones representing the physical internment, with the graces and gifts that God has given us through this pastoral setting, and the animals and people, who will end up in heaven. To me it's a very important, peaceful vision. That's what I'm seeing here: a life of work, activity, education, worship, and finally ending in there being a life after this one.

the brass ring came my way, I was prepared, and I grabbed it.

If I had a lot of money to give to one cause, I'd endeavor to see that young people in America get a sound education, as well as a basing in the moral Judeo-Christian predicate of our country. We have so many freedoms in America because those freedoms are predicated on the idea that citizens will respect one another's person, and one another's property. What happens all too frequently is a breakdown in this respect. While the freedoms are maintained, respect for those freedoms is not.

I think we live in a wonderful country. It's impressed me even more profoundly since taking the job as chairman of the Republican National Committee, and realizing how good most Americans are, and how blessed we are with this democracy, this real freedom we have to do what we want.

My ideal world would be a world of democratic countries, with capitalistic economic systems, that create entrepreneurial opportunities for people to have dreams and hopes that they themselves fulfill. It would also be a world free of dictators who exploit the people they're governing.

I'm optimistic because we're fixing the welfare system in this country, reversing forty years of entrenched central bureaucratic government that I think has taken a lot of meaning out of the lives of many people. And we're giving them more opportunities to have a meaningful life, a life of work and productivity with the self-satisfaction that comes from that. We're also going to improve the education system in America. We're going to empower parents to finally have their choice over how and where their kids go to school, and that's going to make a tremendous difference. I feel very optimistic about the future.

You know, in spite of the dysfunctional nature of my childhood, the turmoil, tension, and insecurity of my upbringing, there was also a pastoral quality about it. And that's something I still long for, a pastoral environment. The vision I have of that is simple; it's not opulent.   *April 3, 1998*

Eleanor HOLMES NORTON

(D-DC), *Delegate, U.S. House of Representatives (since 1996)*

Congresswoman Eleanor Holmes Norton has represented the District of Columbia in the U.S. House of Representatives since 1996. She serves in the Democratic House Leadership Group and previously served as Democratic cochair of the Women's Caucus. She is also a tenured professor of law at Georgetown University and has served on the boards of three *Fortune* 500 companies, the Rockefeller Foundation, and several national civil rights organizations. During the Carter administration she was chair of the Equal Employment Opportunity Commission.

I would hope that somehow war could be made impossible. Actually, I think nuclear war did become impossible. So I don't think that's an idle wish. Once we created meganuclear powers, nuclear war became impossible, ironically and counterintuitively. I would have liked it to have happened another way, but it may well have been what saved us. Now we've got to find a way to make sure that nuclear war doesn't break out at a level way below the superpowers. If we solve that problem, I'd move on to say that war of any kind should be made impossible.

War is such an irrational thing. If you disagree with somebody, you hit them. Wow, what a stupid way to solve a problem. But essentially that's what war is.

I would also hope that women had access to whatever it takes to control their own fertility. That alone could change the world. There's an active correlation in developing countries between how much education a woman has and her view of how many children she should have.

Now in the developing world, women do all the work. It's as if men were still the hunters, and women were reapers, except that being a reaper means you're virtually a slave.

In order for women to control their fertility, they have to believe that they don't need many children to help them gather and plant. And, of course, how many mouths there are to feed has an effect on the devastation of the environment and development itself. Changing the status of women turns out to be fundamental to changing the world. Changing men's status is important if they're

My home is where I find peace, but I would hate to paint an image of the nice easy chair I sit in to work. (I do everything from that chair.) The only thing I can think of is that I've been noticing recently that the city has lots of trees. For most of my life the trees just had leaves, and now I see that the trees go through stages. There's a time when they're little, a time when they're intermediate, and a time when they're full grown. Recently I started paying attention to that, and I like it. Everything is in flux.

poor, but it really won't change the world. Educating women will.

Everything is in flux. Nobody knows anymore what a family is or what it should do. No one knows who the authority figures are. I see all kinds of terrible things that I don't see solutions for, like the state of the black family. How in the world will we ever get to the point where black children have fathers and mothers again?

I want to see people learn how to manage their freedom. I've spent my whole life trying to generate more freedom, and there's never been a society with as much freedom as there is now. And yet that freedom has produced outrageous consequences. So the real question is, Can we instill enough responsibility in people so that they know how to manage freedom?

Can we figure out a way to preserve childhood while affording the maximum amount of freedom to adults? As far as I'm concerned, that's the major challenge to a society that's finally gotten maximum freedom. Now that anybody can get divorced, how do you make people want to stay together? Or understand that parents have responsibilities for children? We solved the freedom issues; now we've got to solve the responsibility issues.

Are there many ways to be a responsible parent? No. There are only a few ways to be a responsible parent. Among them is to spend time with your child. There's no way to avoid that. A good way around this for some people is to face the reality that just because everybody has genitals, and most people are fertile, doesn't mean that everybody ought to be a parent.

People are going back to spirituality because they can see that we haven't managed freedom ourselves, so they hope to erect authority figures again to help us manage it. I think religion helps instill responsibility in people. I mean, it often has that effect.

Personally, I have always found Jesus to be the most extraordinary historical figure. No human being has had a greater effect. But I find dilemmas in Christianity that are at odds with Jesus. For example, the notion that only people who accept Christ can go to heaven. That isn't very Jesus-like. In fact, the most attractive thing about Jesus was the way he reached out to everyone, even those with the least belief. And it doesn't make sense to condemn people who believe in Buddha or Mohammed or any other religious figure.

I think religion has both served and done great disservice to the world. It's divided people in the worst ways. It's responsible for more war than any other single factor. Yet where would we be if there were no system of beliefs constraining human behavior? In the United States, can we find ways to help people control their own behavior? That's the great challenge of our century.

When I was appointed by President Carter to chair the Equal Employment Opportunity Commission at a time when it was a wreck, I tried to bring it back to life. To me and to everybody who looked at it back then, it was an important achievement. But would I want that on my tombstone?

In one sense I think of both of my children as achievements. I have a son who graduated from college and who now earns his own living. And I have a daughter who was born with Down's syndrome. When my husband (now divorced) and I had our daughter, educated though we were (both lawyers), we didn't know a thing about Down's syndrome. But when I thought about it in the weeks that passed, it seemed to me to be justice that we would get this child. If you think of the law of averages, a certain number of Down's syndrome babies will be born. And I thought fate struck in the right place because she was born to two people who had managed through good fortune to get the best education possible in America, and who had lifelong earnings that could support any number of children like this. We also had family who would accept her. So it made sense for this child to be born to me. And of course I instinctively loved her. Raising her was a natural obligation that has turned out to be a joy.

May 9, 1997

Roselyn O'CONNELL

President, National Women's Political Caucus
(1999–2003)

124

Roselyn O'Connell was elected president of the National Women's Political Caucus in 1999, becoming the first Republican to hold that office in over fourteen years. She is in frequent demand throughout the United States and around the world as a speaker and workshop leader on topics related to the involvement of women in the political process.

The first thing I hope for is to see more gender parity, with women in elected and appointed offices, and a woman serving as president of the United States.

I came to this concern at a very, very early age, probably when I was four or five. My sense of the world back then was that women had no power, and I really resented that. I was cognizant of the fact that I was smarter than most boys. I was also the best baseball player on the team; I was excellent at riding horses; I was very brave. And yet I was always in the background, not appreciated. So I knew that wasn't right.

When the National Women's Political Caucus began, issues like day care and health care for women weren't on anybody's agenda. The women's community called these women's issues, but they're really issues that all of society needs to be concerned with. There's also no question that women deal with these issues differently than men do. When women get elected, they tend to make these issues priorities, and fight for them. I'm a pro-choice Republican, and I know that Republican women are just as concerned about these things as women of the other party. I always say that we have a lot more in common as women than we have differences.

I think bringing people out of poverty should be a top priority in our society. We need to make the basics available first, and then education, which is the salvation of society. My idea would be to make classes available, bring professors in every Friday so that anyone who comes to these

I have a vision. The first thing in my ideal world is diversity, which I'm going to represent in the most obvious way, with skin color. But the difference is really in individual skills and strengths. I also need an animal—as much diversity as possible. Also, in my ideal world, there's a thriving, verdant environment, which I'll symbolize by this grass. (If I get a chance to go barefoot on grass, my shoes come off immediately.) Another thing is that everybody has sustenance. But the most important thing in my ideal world is community. One thing we miss in Arizona is porches. (What we have instead is the almighty garage.) In my ideal world every house would have a porch. They're community builders. It's about getting to know your neighbor, in order to recognize the humanity in all of us. And the figures are reaching for one another, because we all need one another. The only other thing I need is a tree, because I love trees. There. I feel really complete with this image.

classes can learn whatever they need. Providing day care might be part of it. We have empty and unused buildings—our public schools—that we really ought to use from 6:00 A.M. until 9:00 or 10:00 at night for things like day care and adult education. Look at what's out there already, and figure out how to get that resource to the people who need it, primarily in education. It's definitely not about just giving them a ten-dollar bill.

What's lacking, especially for women who may be single moms, is the feeling that "I could do that." Their entire existence is bound up in providing housing, feeding their children, and getting clothes on their backs. A person has time to think about other things only if they've got the basics covered. There are too many people, and the majority of them unfortunately are women and children, who don't have the luxury of focusing on higher things because the basics are so questionable for them. I have a lot of empathy for that.

I am so awestruck sometimes by what women who don't have advantages are able to do. They're marginalized in so many ways. We need to figure out how to equalize things, and in my opinion the best way to do that is to get women elected who have compassion, and who know what the hell it's like.

I was a single mom for four years with three boys, which was very challenging. The older I get the more I realize that raising those boys was probably the most significant work I'll ever do. At the time I didn't know that. If I had, I would have paid more attention. I wasn't watching the little things they did, and I feel sad about that. There's a miracle there, and I took it for granted. You get so bound up in what you're doing at the moment that you don't look and appreciate.

The other thing is that I've had the distinct pleasure of working with young women who are very smart, and a lot of them are true feminists. Their attitude is, "What do you mean I can't take time off to take my kids to the doctor?" I mean, they just won't have any of it, and I'm really encouraged by that.

Some of the younger women have no idea how difficult it was to get reproductive rights, and of course that battle is far from over. But trying to engage young women in that is really difficult. A lot of them are just clueless. They don't understand that it used to be against the law to take birth control pills, and you couldn't get them unless you were married, and even then the doctor got to decide if you could have them or not. It's just awesome when you think about where we were thirty years ago, and even though we're nowhere near where we want to be, we've made some progress.

July 19, 2001

Clarence PAGE

Pulitzer Prize–winning Columnist and Editorial Board Member, The Chicago Tribune _(since 1984)_

Clarence Page has been a columnist and member of the editorial board of _The Chicago Tribune_ since 1984. He won a Pulitzer Prize for commentary written for that newspaper in 1989. (His column is now syndicated nationally by Tribune Media Services.) He is also a news analyst for ABC's _This Week,_ a regular contributor to _NewsHour with Jim Lehrer_ (PBS), and a frequent panelist on Black Entertainment Television (BET).

My image of an ideal world is one in which every individual has an equal opportunity to actualize themselves. And the only way they can have that is through adequate education. That's essential. It comes hard behind the basic necessities of food, clothing, and shelter.

We have enough food to feed the world right now; we just aren't doing it because of politics, pure and simple. Whenever you run into starvation crises, they're always caused by politics, and that's been true for decades. And for everything else—clothing, shelter, and education—I think it's true, too. We have the ability to give equal opportunity to everyone in the world; it's just that politics gets in the way. So I'd like to see a world in which politics was less of a hindrance and more of a facilitator.

I'm optimistic about the direction we're going in the long run. It's the short term I'm worried about. The end of the Cold War was a good thing, but every time an empire breaks apart, the formerly colonized sections turn against one another. We see that all over Africa and in Latin America. When the colonial powers pulled out, old tribal animosities came back—Yugoslavia, Azerbaijan, Russia, Ukraine—and it's happening right now in the United States, too. The end of the Cold War has seen the rise of militia groups, and a rise in interethnic and interracial tensions.

I've been looking at American history, though, and for all its diversity this country is remarkably flexible. We're not Bosnia or Azerbaijan, or Northern Ireland. Many Americans like to be the Chicken Littles who raise the red flag and say, "Watch out, we're going to become another Quebec."

I'm a city guy. I grew up in a small town but was always eager to move to a big city, because I liked the variety, the excitement, the diversity, the high level of tolerance, the right amount of choices it offered, and the intellectual vitality. My ideal world would probably look like a UNICEF card.

Isn't it funny that for someone who wasn't that enamored of nature, I painted a pristine natural environment for my ideal world? I was thinking of the broad diversity of the world's people all getting along, and having a clean environment that we can all enjoy. This is coming close to my childhood view of heaven. When I think of the way I want the world to be, I think about how people ought to live, and what their environment ought to be like. So that's what this represents.

We can never be another Quebec, because we don't have the same history as Quebec. We're a very different country. We're flexible and diverse. And basically I think we're people not just with good intentions but also with good intelligence on the whole.

Americans have always been schizophrenic about real diversity, though. The Founding Fathers (and they were fathers, you know, white men) had wonderful words about equal opportunity but didn't practice those words. Same thing is true in Japan right now. That's not a country accustomed to diversity, and yet they've got it. Internationally they say they love diversity, but they don't recognize it in their domestic society. I think the whole world is catching on to diversity—it creeps in and before you know it you're diverse. It's happening.   *March 12, 1997*

Nancy PELOSI

(D-CA), Member, U.S. House of Representatives (since 1987); House Democratic Whip (since 2002)

Nancy Pelosi (D-CA) has represented the San Francisco district in the U.S. House of Representatives since 1987. She became House Democratic Whip in January 2002, making her the highest-ranking woman in congressional history. She is a member of the House Appropriations Committee and the ranking Democrat on the House Permanent Select Committee on Intelligence. Pelosi is known for her support of bills to increase funding for AIDS/HIV and breast cancer research, and for U.S. leadership on human rights and sustainable development.

I hope, as we go into the next century, that we leave behind us some of the terrible baggage of this last century in terms of Communism, Nazism, and all kinds of authoritarianism. The twentieth century from beginning to end was a bloody mess in terms of human rights.

There isn't a speech in Congress, or at NATO, or the UN, in which people don't talk about human rights, and respect for the dignity of every person. But then they're inconsistent. "Business is involved; we can't change the world." If a political goal is involved, we use force. I think if we're consistent about the value of every person, that spark of divinity that we say exists in every person, then we can't tolerate what's happening in Africa or anyplace where people's dignity is not being respected.

I would like to see a world where that value is respected. But to get from here to there, we have to stop the hypocrisy. We have to wed ourselves to a set of principles, like the Universal Declaration of Human Rights. We must honor it. We have to put our ideals before our deals.

I love the freedom of a tightly knit idea. Whether it's raising my family, or my political work. What are the decisions we've made as a family? How will we go forward? And now let everyone be as spontaneous as they want to be within an agreed-upon set of priorities. I like to bring people together, establish priorities, and then let a thousand flowers blossom.

The district I represent is the most magnificent district there is. I'm sure every member of Congress believes that, but in my case it's true. As they say of San Francisco, my constituency, the

This painting has a horizon because horizons remind us that we may not always succeed. I remember that Vaclav Havel talked about democracy being a horizon, something we're always striving for. So we're never satisfied. We'll always find newer horizons to improve the situation. And the closer we get, the higher our standards will be. The perfectibility of man is part of my religion. I'm a Catholic.

This ideal world is also going to have a blue sky, and a cloud. Just as a sign of something going on—life. And it's going to have a green island, which is going to be like the environment. This is the water, which is life, and new horizons, whether that means just being adventurous or not being dissatisfied if you haven't reached all your goals. So we've protected the environment, the great ocean is a source of life, the blue sky is for happiness, and there's a horizon to strive for. It's about endless prospects. Go for it! Get where you're going, and realize there's a lot more to do, and that everyone doesn't get there at the same time.

It took great resistance for me not to draw the great big eyes of my grandchildren. This painting is all about them, and not just my grandchildren, the next generation.

beauty is in the mix. We have this incredible diversity, every kind of person.

The second thing I would hope for in my ideal world is that we understand that war should be obsolete. It's not a civilized way to resolve differences. And we now know that the environment pays a tremendous price.

I think people will be on the right side of the future when they start to recognize the importance of the environment in everything we do. You can't talk about trade, commerce, war, or anything, unless you consider first what this means for the air we breathe, the water we drink, the sustainability of our environment. It's not an elitist idea; it's fundamental. *May 25, 1999*

John J. PHELAN, JR.

Chairman and CEO, New York Stock Exchange, (1984–90)

John J. Phelan, Jr., was part of the senior management of the New York Stock Exchange (NYSE) from 1975 to 1990, first as vice chairman, then as president, finally as chairman and CEO. During his tenure he laid the foundation for the use of modern information technology by the exchange and built the NYSE into a leading international financial institution. He was appointed chairman of the Private Sector Initiative by President Reagan and helped reestablish the stock exchanges of both China and the former Soviet Union. Phelan is best known for his steady handling of the financial markets during the stock market meltdown of 1987. He served as president of the International Federation of Stock Market Exchanges from 1991 to 1993.

What I hope for is a very prosperous country, in which all elements of society participate without relying on government aid. I also hope we find ways to provide great incentives for people to work, and to take care of those who drop through the cracks, without totally socializing this country. We need to build on our educational platform. There are different ideas about what educated means, but one is that you're at least literate and can do the fundamentals.

I worked with the first Mrs. Bush on her literacy foundation, and that was a big problem in this country in the late '80s, early '90s. People came to this country from all over the world for our graduate education, but our basic primary and secondary education had real problems. So I would hope to correct that.

Also, of course, home defense. Absolutely. I believe in taking care of the United States before you take care of the rest of the world, and we've got a lot to take care of here right now. The good thing is that in the last ten years we've begun to pay down the debt we made in the 1980s. The bad thing is that it's like asking everybody what they want for Christmas, and everybody wants at least ten things.

Now it's back down to where this country has to decide on one or two things to do, and in every social contract, whether it's Locke or Rousseau, the first thing is national defense. That's what citizens cannot do by themselves. Now I don't know how much money should be spent on that, but it obviously should be more than we're spending now.

133

The professional finance world that I worked in for forty years was very exciting but also very high stress. Trading may be high stress, but money management is stressful at a different level. We had responsibility for whole institutions.

I remember that by the early 1980s we were trying to redefine the New York Stock Exchange and explain to people that it wasn't just about stocks and bonds. We were raising money so it would be invested in the economy to help it grow. We were about people's future, their pension funds.

Then at some point I began to think that if America was the only reasonably prosperous country, we had a problem. So how could we help other countries help themselves? By introducing them to market-driven economies.

In the People's Republic of China, Deng Xiaoping was looking for ways to veer off the traditional Communist model. Communism wasn't working, and in the early '80s everybody wanted to talk to the chairman at the largest stock exchange. We were invited to talk to the Chinese about how they could improve their markets.

So in 1986 I took a delegation of twenty-five people involved in markets, foreign currency, and commodity trading to Beijing, and we held a four-day seminar in the People's Bank of China. They asked us what we thought about capitalism, and I said we think we have a good model, which is not perfect, but it seems to work better than most others. It's a balance between raw capitalism and socialism. And I told them that the purpose of a market-driven

economy is to raise the standard of living for all our people. I said, "What we're trying to do in our country and what you're trying to do in your country is raise the standard of living for all. So we have a common goal, and we can work from that."

So we helped reopen the Chinese stock exchange in Shanghai. I spent an hour and a half with Deng Xiaoping, and we talked about regulations and how to protect investors, how he should set up enterprise zones and let China feel its way toward a market-driven economy. He was willing to experiment, and the Chinese, of course, think in aeons. He was eighty-two years old, and yet he wanted to talk about the next hundred years. So that was very successful.

I did a lot of work in this country and overseas to convince people that communism and socialism had been a failure in Europe and the East. President Reagan had something called private sector initiatives, and I was chairman of that board. We did programs in Europe, all focused on encouraging people to depend less on government and to be more entrepreneurial. And, being more entrepreneurial, to create organizations that would create jobs and hopefully raise the standard of living in the whole country.

In 1990 I took another group to Russia and talked to Gorbachev, which was very difficult. The Chinese understand trade and money and business, but in those days the Russians didn't. So no matter what we said, they would ask, "But when does the government fix the *price*?"

Europe is kind of a hybrid. They migrated off from socialism

For goodness' sake, they'll think a four-year-old kid did this painting. Actually, I came in second in the national finger-painting contest when I was in the third grade! It was fantastic! But that was it. I peaked out. I haven't been creative ever since.

This painting has both day and night. We've got a lovely garden with the city around it. What I'm trying for is tranquillity and, at the same time, industry. A balance. I'll put in a stick figure reading a book, and something over here that reflects health and prosperity. Rising up out of this garden is somebody reading. Here's a symbol for education, and the double helix or the cross for medicine. Then, for prosperity, a dollar sign. (I wish I had another symbol for prosperity, but I'm missing one at the moment.) Prosperity in the city, and a garden for contemplation.

135

just as we migrated off from capitalism, and now everybody's trying to find some mix where you can stimulate the economy and provide jobs without killing the initiative of people.

Another one of my top priorities for any society would be medical care, particularly for people who are young or old, or for those who drop through the cracks. Some way has to be found to help those people. If you can't get excellent medical care to everybody, at least get some medical care to everybody. The trick is to bring some people up without bringing the whole system down. A similar problem exists in education. We've tried to provide a university education for everyone, and so have failed on the primary and secondary levels.

When I was young I hated the city, but as I've gotten older I like to go to cities and see what man has created. I'm interested in seeing how people live in groups, how they help each other, how they grow and attack problems. I also love to go to churches to see how people express themselves in relation to whatever Supreme Being they believe in. I think in times of unease and terror people are drawn back to faith. When times are good, we all think they're going to stay good. There's the old saying on Wall Street that a bull market breeds nothing but geniuses. I think that's true of life, too. Things are going well, and you think you're really smart.

I've been lucky, but then I've always had a plan. It's like a ship that leaves port with some destination in mind. It may get blown off course, or it may decide to change its destination in midstream, but it's got to start with a goal. That's true with life, and with business, too.

September 20, 2001

Sally QUINN

Washington Political Author and Commentator

Sally Quinn has been known in the nation's capital as a shrewd, sophisticated, and witty observer of American political and cultural life for over twenty years. She writes frequently for *The Washington Post* and is also the author of several books, including her most recent, *The Party: A Guide to Adventurous Entertaining* (1997).

I have a very strong sense of place, where I am and how it looks, the aesthetics of my environment. I feel that I have to be able to look out and sense water nearby. Georgetown appeals to me aesthetically almost more than any place I've ever been. It's like a little village within a city. I like to be where the action is, to be able to walk out the door and have restaurants and movie theaters and shops close by. I find New York City very exciting, too, but I wouldn't like living there, or anyplace where there are skyscrapers. The worst place for me would be a suburb.

Another thing I like about living near Washington is the whole notion of being where there is power. I like to study power; I like to observe it—people who don't have power and want it; people who get power and abuse it. What happens to people when they start losing power? And after they lose it, how do they behave? How do they try to get it back? Those questions pertain to almost any relationship, whether between husband and wife or parent and child, but they're all magnified in government.

Certainly everyone hopes there will be peace everywhere. You think about the Middle East. But I think that's a symptom of what is the biggest, most important problem everywhere, which is over-population. In fifty years, if we don't control the population, we're going to lose the planet. It will be overdevelopment, destruction of the environment, lack of resources, a total disaster.

It's a very tricky issue. There are a lot of Catholic countries that don't believe in birth control, and a lot of countries that don't believe in abortion. Although abortion is not everyone's number-one, favorite method of birth control, it is an important method of birth control. I just think it's very unrealistic to think that without abortion, and without a very serious effort to control population, we're not going to be living in a nightmare in a few decades. The most important thing is to educate women.

Right now there are people who scoff at the whole idea of overpopulation, even though it's *the* problem of the environment and everything else. Why is there crime in the streets? Because people are poor, and having babies they don't want and can't take care of. So the children have no parents and grow up running in the streets, without money, without any kind of supervision, and without any values. So, whatever issue you pinpoint and say, "This is a problem," it all comes down to population, or teen pregnancy, which is a population problem. If we control the human population, we can probably save the planet; if we don't, we won't.

That said, the most rewarding thing I've ever done personally is raising my child, who is severely learning disabled. He's fine, but he's had a lot of serious medical problems, physical problems, and now severe learning disabilities. It's been an enormous challenge to make sure he has confidence in himself.

I felt very good one night when the three of us were having dinner, and he took a big gulp of milk, put his glass down, and said, "I just love my life." I thought, I can't believe that someone with the kinds of problems he has could say that, so that was very heartening to me. There are so many setbacks and so many disappointments every day. But when he said, "I love my life," it felt like it was all worthwhile, all of the heartaches and hardships we've experienced over the last fifteen years.   *September 15, 1997*

I don't think I've ever had a paintbrush in my hand. Now I know what it feels like to be learning disabled.

This is extremely amateurish, but my image of a perfect world is a mother and child sitting on the beach looking at this beautiful, clean ocean and beautiful, clean sky and beautiful, clear sunlight. Of course, that will only happen if we manage to get the population under control, because otherwise we're not going to have clean water and clean air. So this is the mother and the son sitting on the beach, and they're very happy. He's playing with his little bucket and shovel, and it's clean sand, and they're basically enjoying the environment. It's a situation I've actually been in. It's me and Quinn.

Robert C. RICHARDSON

Nobel Laureate (Physics, 1996); Floyd R. Newman Professor of Physics, Vice Provost for Research, Cornell University

Robert C. Richardson is Floyd R. Newman Professor of Physics, director of the Laboratory of Atomic and Solid State Physics, and vice provost for Research at Cornell University. He was awarded the Nobel Prize in physics (along with David Lee and Douglas Osheroff) in 1996, for research on liquid 3He, which they discovered undergoes a pairing transition similar to that of superconductors.

I'm basically a happy person who gets along pretty well as long as I have a warm place and food I like to eat. I guess in my perfect world I'd like to know what I know now but have the heart and lungs and body weight, and teeth, of a twenty-year-old.

I like a certain amount of intellectual stimulation and also some free and unfettered time to follow my pursuits. A university setting is paradise for me; I've been here at Cornell for thirty-two years, and I'm very committed to universities. I think, in the right circumstances, university education and research can be the most effective investments for the future survivability of the world. That's where new knowledge is generated.

I researched the work that led to the Nobel Prize a long time ago, but I remember that as an extremely rewarding thing. We knew we had discovered something that had really fascinating and unusual properties, and the whole business of tracking it down was very exciting. I've felt that way only a couple of other times in research.

My first priority for the world is population stabilization without any major disruptions like war and disease, which would be awful ways to get to population stabilization. I want some broader understanding of what a sustainable environment is, so that we can have a reasonable hope that life can continue indefinitely. I also want the majority of the world to have a better standard of living. And, of course, all those things are contingent on world peace, and a society that can survive, propagate, and continue on indefinitely.

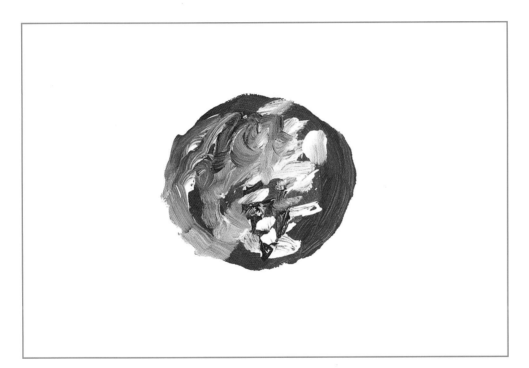

I'm a very poor freehand graphic artist, and I'm also color-blind, so those are a lot more colors than I wanted to consider.

What I'm painting here is the planet Earth, and I'm going to show an ocean and an atmosphere. The important thing is that the atmosphere is livable, the oceans are clean, and life on Earth is thriving. That's the first thing that occurred to me—the image of Earth from space.

141

My personal belief is not in a god that's humanlike. But I do recognize that there was a beginning to the universe, and that something ignited it. I know I can't answer those questions. But it's fun seeing what we can answer. I'm increasingly aware that some of the most interesting things in astronomy and astrophysics, for instance, can change the way people understand the universe, how it got started and where it's going. I found those Voyager pictures of the moons of Jupiter incredibly exciting, these beautiful color pictures showing volcanoes on the surface. The things we learn from measurements of objects halfway across the universe can affect people's religion in fundamental ways.

The big bang is something that when I was in college people would not have dreamed of. "Only religious nuts believe in that," we would have said. But there's strong evidence that everything we know started off at one point, and one time. We discovered that through deep skepticism, careful experiments, and measuring things. It wasn't through religious conviction in advance. So what could be more profound?

We're also at a time right now when people primarily in the physical sciences and engineering are developing new instrumentation for looking at the most microscopic levels of life. And there's a recognition that there has been at least four billion years of evolution, during which nature optimized how everything worked, not only in human beings but in grasshoppers, and birds, and fish, and plants. Now we can take those things apart and do reverse engineering on what nature spent four billion years putting together. There are remarkable things that will come out of that that will certainly affect human beings in very deep ways.

Then, there's the possibility of major changes as a consequence of information technologies. It's possible to build hundreds of thousands of little detectors that sense everything that's going on. So you could have a society in which there's a benign way to make everything work a whole lot better. It's called intelligent infrastructure. That could be very, very different, and it could be very bad. Imagine, say, a central authority that has thousands and thousands of tiny, inexpensive video cameras everywhere, that see where everyone's going. It's Orwell's worst nightmare. So it could work both ways.

My family has been very important to me, my daughters growing up. I had two daughters, but one died four years ago at the age of twenty-eight, of cardiac arrest. It was a sudden, shocking thing. I think nothing can affect a human being more than the death of a child, and that's probably built in genetically. I mean, I was deeply saddened by the death of my parents, but it seemed like a natural thing. When it happens the other way around, the grief is much deeper, and you feel a level of despair that you just couldn't predict.

February 15, 1999

Alice RIVLIN

*Vice Chair, U.S. Federal Reserve System
(1996–99); Director, White House Office of
Management and Budget (1994–96); Founding
Director, Congressional Budget Office (1973–83)*

Alice Rivlin is Henry J. Cohen Professor of Urban Management and Policy at the New School University and a senior fellow at the Brookings Institution. She served as vice chair of the U.S. Federal Reserve from 1996 to 1999, and as director of the White House Office of Management and Budget from 1994 to 1996. Rivlin was also the founding director of the Congressional Budget Office and president of the American Economic Association. She is a frequent contributor to newspapers, television, and radio, and the author of several books.

I hope for a world where there is much less violence. I don't imagine that there will ever be none. But that would be my first desire for the world. I would also hope for more opportunity for more children. Most American children are very fortunate by world standards, and some American children are very fortunate even by American standards. They have opportunities to make something of their lives. I would like to see that for more children. That's what a growing economy does for you.

I'd like to take a piece of an inner city and see whether we could get all of the children in that area into better situations in their lives. Exactly how, I don't know. It's hard. Building a better community where things are really bad is not just a question of building better schools or better housing, or even getting people to work together in the neighborhood. It's all those things together.

I think what you don't do is go in and give people things. That's a mistake a lot of people make. I was talking recently to some computer company executives who wanted to just give people computers. Making that work depends very heavily on finding good people in the community to teach other people how to use those resources, and to organize a self-help effort that they can then support. Just to dump some nice buildings into an area and imagine that good things will happen from that is wrong.

Economics is on the whole a very difficult thing to get right, and there probably isn't any "right" in an absolute sense. I think economists know a lot more than they did a few decades ago,

143

but one of the things they know is that things are more complicated than we once thought. Simple theories don't work.

I guess my personal wish is that people learn better how to communicate with one another, that there would be less misunderstanding and more positive human interaction. A lot of people aren't very good parents. It may not always be their fault; nobody helped them. I see so many parental problems, and marriage problems, and neighbor problems. A lot of people just don't think much about how to build better relationships in their family, or in their community. There are misunderstandings, and people who probably could get along if they just thought more about it, don't. They need better interpersonal skills.

I am very optimistic, though. My husband and I joke about this because I usually think things will work out, and he often doesn't. I'm right sometimes, and not other times. But I don't spend time worrying about downside risk, as we say.

I'm also more confident at this stage in my life, and less afraid of new things. I have just been a beneficiary of two miracles of medicine. I had cataract surgery and also a hip replacement, which

was terrific. I'm much better off than a sixty-seven-year-old woman with similar problems would have been thirty years ago.

A lot of things have changed in my lifetime, and I think that change will go on happening. But most big changes have both positive and negative sides. The communications revolution is wonderful in some ways. I can e-mail my grandchildren, or whatever. But, it's also giving us information overload, which is a very challenging thing to live with. Actually, I am not extremely anxious to see what the next phase is.

Longer life seems like an attractive thing as long as one can go on doing positive things with the extra time. I like getting things done, finished, achieved. I like to be busy; I like to have responsibility; I like interacting with people. I also like to get outdoors; I do a lot of mountain hiking. One of my favorite places to do that is in Nepal. We camped there one night, and it was maybe the most spectacular and beautiful place I've ever been. I also remember a particularly beautiful place in Peru, where we came up over a mountain to look down on a really clear, beautiful blue lake. That was wonderful.

June 2, 1998

Beautiful paints, wonderful colors! This is going to be fun. I never get a chance to do this. So, these are mountains; this is a lake; this is a house with a deck. I really wanted to put my grandchildren in here. That's what these bright colors represent. Maybe I'll put them on the deck, and they're about to get on a sailboat. This picture is sort of a composite. It's like a place we go to in Vermont on Lake Champlain, where we rent a little house. The Adirondack Mountains are not that close; they're across the lake, on the New York side.

This was an enormous amount of fun. I'm sorry I don't draw better, but . . . I've done crayons with my granddaughter, but you don't have to be very skilled to do that.

145

General H. Norman SCHWARZKOPF

Commander in Chief, U.S. Central Command,
Commander of Allied Forces, Gulf War
(1990–91)

General H. Norman Schwarzkopf is best known as commander in chief, U.S. Central Command, and commander of Allied Forces during the Gulf War (Desert Shield and Desert Storm) in 1990 and '91. His military career included service as deputy commander of the Joint Task Force in charge of U.S. forces in Grenada and two combat tours in Vietnam. He holds a Congressional Gold Medal and the Presidential Medal of Freedom. Now retired, Schwarzkopf is the author of the best-selling autobiography *It Doesn't Take a Hero* (1993) and cochairman (with Steven Spielberg) of STARBRIGHT, a program devoted to improving the lives of seriously ill children.

It's easy for me to say what I hope for in the world: No more war! I mean, human beings have got to find a better way of solving their differences than killing one another. People lose sight of the fact that there are about thirty wars going on out there all the time. There are all sorts of wars along disputed borders, and religious wars, that sort of thing. I'm convinced that wars aren't the answer to anything; they're temporary solutions. All they do is build up animosity, which later comes bubbling up again, just as is happening in Bosnia and Kosovo. So, if we could come to our senses and recognize that you don't solve anything by killing each other, that would be what I would look for.

I have been very, very lucky to have lived all over the world. Actually, the five years I spent in Europe as a teenager, coupled with my four years at West Point, probably molded 99 percent of my value system. In Europe, I was exposed to so many different cultures, and so many of them have been around much longer than we have, and we can learn from them. Yet I came home with the greatest love ever for the United States of America. I don't mean to pat myself on the back, but when I came back to the United States, I was a straight-A student and valedictorian of my class, because my horizons had been expanded so much. Then when I went to West Point, I was exposed for four years to a culture that taught duty, honor, and country. With a lot of my classmates, that message didn't take; but I believed it. I absorbed it. It became my value system for life.

If I had a lot of extra money to spend on one cause, I'd give it to the huge umbrella of education,

For someone who has no artistic talent whatsoever, this assignment is wonderful. Boy, this is a big challenge. The only thing to do is just jump right in, right? You just kind of have to go with it. It's an emotional experience.

What I'm thinking of in this painting is a kind of universal well-being. I really want it to be a scene of tranquillity, a scene of happiness, a scene of peace. And I want it to be for everything; I want it to be for men, women, animals, fish, and whatever else happens to be out there. I can honestly say that, on a personal level, I'm happiest when I'm out in the wilderness, or just surrounded by the beauty of nature. I'll never forget when I went fly-fishing in Alaska for the very first time. I flew in a little two-seater airplane, and we landed on the shore of this lake. When the engine went off, the silence came across the lake and smacked us in the side of the head. I guess the serenity is what I really, truly enjoy. These things in the painting are all things I love. I love bears; I love the outdoors; I love fish; I love the mountains. Sort of a selfish picture, I guess.

which would allow me to take care of a lot of problems at once. I'm convinced that prejudice is learned, so it can be unlearned. Cancer can be cured, if we become educated and smart enough to do it. Through education, people can come to understand that you can't accomplish anything by killing each other. Maybe we can even teach the value of selfless service through education.

I think a lot of what's happening today with children in the computer world is wonderful. They can be exposed to all sorts of things they otherwise would never have been exposed to. I'm convinced that the demise of the Soviet Union did not come about because of a failure of communism as much as by the fact that, all of a sudden, all those people in Russia were exposed through new information channels to what was going on in the rest of the world, and they suddenly decided that communism wasn't really that great. So I hope this international communication will bring us closer together, and help us solve our problems.

People ask me what my proudest accomplishments are, and I think they expect me to say winning the Gulf War. My proudest accomplishments are my three kids; they are wonderful human beings. That's what I like about them. They care about other people, and they're very sensitive. I am very proud of all three of them.

The Gulf War was also a rewarding experience, because we were able to get it over with, with so few casualties. We had been through Vietnam and were able to purge ourselves of the evils of that war, get the ground war over in a very few days, with very low casualties.

Actually, one of the most rewarding experiences of my life was my first tour in Vietnam, in 1965 and '66, when I was an adviser to Vietnamese paratroopers. We spent most of our time out in the jungles involved in military operations. Where they went, I went; where they slept, I slept; what they ate, I ate. I lost a huge amount of weight; I got malaria and amoebic dysentery. But it was one of the most rewarding experiences of my life because I honestly felt I was serving something other than myself—the cause of democracy. These people were fighting for the freedom of their country, and I was helping them do that, for which I received nothing tangible in return. It was selfless service, and it was a wonderful experience.

Some people say it sounds trite, but I believe the single most important concept in the world is selfless service. I honestly believe that that's where true happiness lies. Every time I've been involved in that sort of service, I've been the happiest. And I honestly believe that if you could just teach the children of the world one thing, it should be selfless service.

One thing I love about the United States of America is that you can do your own thing. That's wonderful. But I would like everyone in this country to do their own thing, plus one. Do your own thing, but then just do one other thing to help someone else. What a great world it would be if everyone did their own thing, plus one.

March 22, 1999

Robert SHAPIRO

Chairman and CEO, Monsanto Life Sciences Company (1995–2000); Chairman, Pharmacia Corporation (2000–01)

Robert Shapiro served as chairman and CEO of Monsanto Company from 1995 to 2000 and then chairman of Pharmacia Corporation following the merger of Monsanto, Pharmacia Corporation, and Upjohn. He had previously been president, chairman, and CEO of the NutraSweet Company, a subsidiary of Monsanto. Shapiro was also a member of the President's Advisory Committee on Trade Policy under President Clinton. He received the 1999 Emerging Markets CEO of the Year Award.

When people talk about peak experiences, they usually talk about facing some difficult challenge they weren't sure they could surmount. Usually they did it with others, and ended up doing it in ways that they couldn't have even imagined before, so they found something deep, and valid, and creative, and committed, and passionate in themselves and in the people they worked with.

I had that kind of experience when we started the NutraSweet business. We were introducing a new sweetener into a world that at that time basically had two sweetener alternatives: sugar and saccharin, each of which had some bad issues associated with it. We started out with six people, none of whom had ever done anything like this before. (I had been a law professor and a general counsel before that.) And in about three years, we had about fifteen hundred people and a half-billion-dollar business. It exploded. So we did something that people thought we couldn't, and we turned out to be right. We also did things that turned out to be wrong, but they didn't matter because our momentum was so powerful. It was an incredible ride.

The thing I've found most interesting about corporations, more than government institutions, or universities, or law firms, is that the pace of change is faster, because the payoff for change is immediate. In a political or university environment there isn't any great advantage to being out ahead of change. But in a corporation you have to try to imagine what the future is going to look like, and then figure out what you want to do to either resist the change, adapt to it, or get out ahead. Business is the most complicated game of strategy I've ever encountered. It's a matter of judging people and coming to the right conclusions about complicated situations. That's what I most enjoy.

I also see business as a central part of human experience. Most of us were brought up on the Marxist model that the purpose of management is to exploit labor, and the purpose of labor is to avoid being exploited. Obviously, if that's the case, there's always a hidden tension between the two, and the enterprise as a whole suffers. It's internal warfare. My own experience has been that people want to do work that has value and dignity, and they want to contribute. So if you align what people want for themselves with the goal of the company, it's a pretty powerful model.

Human beings specialize in generalization. We adapt to a lot of different environmental niches, in part because we alter the environment.

There's a profound explosion of knowledge about genes going on right now that will be looked back on as a turning point in human history. It will give us choices about things that previously weren't within the realm of choice.

We're now trying to apply that new knowledge to agriculture. Fundamentally what we're trying to do is what crop breeders have been doing for ten thousand years—breed crops that have desirable characteristics. But now there are ways to get traits that couldn't have been acquired by breeding, traits from other species that could make agriculture more productive and more sustainable. Could

these technologies be used in destructive ways? Yes. Just as chemistry can be used in destructive ways, and has been. The issue is not can it be used badly, but do we have the right controls.

In food safety, there are very well established ways of testing whether something is dangerous for people to eat. With environmental consequences, the issues aren't as clear. The part that's least understood is what would be the implications of genetic changes for biodiversity over time. Those things need study.

Society is going to need to establish ways of testing that say we have reasonable confidence that these products don't create some new, radically different kind of risk. And if we're wrong, the consequences are not likely to be disastrous or irreversible. If you have that kind of regulatory process, then you can say, "Let's proceed step by step."

Around the turn of the last century, when the notion of an automobile began to become conceivable, there were no regulatory processes in place to decide whether someone should be allowed to introduce automobiles. So it just happened. Then it became obvious that if you're introducing automobiles, you've got to build roads. You've got to redesign the way cities work. Suburbs became not just practical but desirable, with consequences for urban cores. Issues of pollution, of accidents, and so on all arose out of that invention. It would have been helpful if there had been some system that could have made an assessment of the impact of this new technology, but things like the urban consequences would have been hard to see.

I will tell you I think agriculture is one field in which the benefits

I know what I want to paint; I actually have a picture in mind. It's a balance between nature and human sophistication and technology. Nature is so complicated these days, because humans have done so much to alter it. But there is a kind of dark, uncontrollable, and endlessly creative nature that's part of my ideal world, a mysterious, deep thing. Then there's a cultivated nature, which I picture as rolling green hills. If I do this right, you'll get this sense of it stretching back, being a large domain where people have made a pleasant place to live. The other thing I picture is a golden city in the hills, much of it actually underground, but you can see the dome part aboveground. The orange is the technology aspect, an intensely human space that needs to be constrained so that it doesn't do a lot of damage. The whole scene is about a peaceful coexistence.

are quite sizable, and the risks are pretty controllable. I think the parts that are going to be complicated will involve higher mammals and people.

Dolly the sheep is a scientific tour de force, but she poses all sorts of complicated ethical issues. Some of them force us to examine, again, our practices in relation to animals. What does it mean to be human and have power over other species?

The question is, Is this all going to be governed by markets? Markets are wonderful tools for wealth creation, and you interfere with markets at some risk, just as you interfere with ecosystems at some risk. Markets and ecosystems are both complex, adaptive systems, but neither of them operate on ethical principles. Markets express human wants in very crude terms. But moral aspirations are things that society has to make conscious choices about.

I was a city kid by birth, and I love cities. I'm in awe of nature, but I don't feel comfortable with it. I know it's needed—it's important materially, spiritually, and in many other ways—but I don't trust it.

That said, the first thing I want for the world is for world population to peak at no more than, say, ten billion. And it has to stay flat or be declining at that point, because having too many people vastly complicates issues. Secondly, I want a world in which technologies allow us to live in an environmentally sustainable way, a way that doesn't degrade the planet's ability to sustain our lives and the lives of other species. Those technologies probably don't exist today, so they have to be developed.

Also, extreme poverty has to be eradicated in a more perfect world, which is not to say that I'm looking for a world of total financial equality. That sort of world wouldn't work. But today there are about two billion people who live in conditions that would not fall within anyone's definition of being humanly acceptable. The nightmare world is one in which there are cities of forty million people or more living in shocking poverty, and islands of wealth that have to defend themselves against the oceans of poverty. That's obviously not ethically acceptable, and it's also politically dangerous.

As long as you have desperate conditions that any person of spirit would say are intolerable, something must change. If it's not going to change peacefully, then it will change by violence. It has to lead to war. Which is not to say that prosperity is a guarantee of peace.

I'm really worried about the next fifty years. I worry about the proliferation of weapons of mass destruction and the democratization of power, so that even very small groups of people can do very great harm to large numbers of people. I worry about the breakdown of political order and of social constraints, the reversion increasingly to fanatical religious passions. You want me to envision a world where it all turns out well, but how did that happen?

August 18, 1999

Alan SIMPSON

(R–WY), Senator, U.S. Senate (1978–97); Director, Institute of Politics, Kennedy School of Government, Harvard University (1998–2000)

Alan Simpson served his home state of Wyoming in the U.S. Senate for eighteen years, ten of them as Senate Republican Whip. He was an active force on the Judiciary Committee, Finance Committee, and Environment and Public Works Committee. In 1998 he became director of the Institute of Politics at the Kennedy School of Government, Harvard University. Two years later, he returned to his home state to lecture in political science at the University of Wyoming.

I have learned to thrive, and I mean that, wherever I am, because that's the only place I am. Sounds corny, doesn't it? I lived in Germany when I was twenty-four years old, and I did not thrive there because I was in the army and it was the first time in my life I couldn't do what I wanted to. But I slowly began to grow up. My father used to say, "Any damned fool can be unhappy." And when, out of self-pity, I felt that I was the human toilet bowl, I decided to stop that. So, the way you do that is not to pretend that there's only one place you can triumph. I mean, do I have to be only at the Bobcat Ranch on a beautiful summer evening in order to thrive? No! But I tell you, I love it when I'm there.

Having said that, of course, the best place of all is the Bobcat Ranch on the south fork of the Shoshone River, outside of Cody, Wyoming. My parents bought that ranch in 1933, and my dear brother and I grew up there, and now his children and my children and grandchildren. One hundred twenty-five acres of pure paradise. Walk around at night, never see a streetlight or car light. Hallowed ground, hallowed ground.

I couldn't possibly pick the most rewarding things in life. I've been sworn into the U.S. Senate, and served there for eighteen years. I've been given every honor they can give. I have three magnificent children. I've been living with the same woman for forty-four years and I still have the hots for her. Now that's a nice way to live.

For the larger world I do hope people will themselves personally deal more honestly with the

153

serious problems that confront the country instead of listening to politicians bullshit them. People who have a marvelous command of the English language get others all worked up about methane gas in cows and propellant in the bottom of shaving cream cans. I commend them for their good works, but it won't do a thing until we deal with the population of the earth. All the rest is applesauce; it means nothing.

Saving your cans or taking your plastic down to the . . . Forget it. The game is already played. From the beginning of man, when we crawled out of sod, to the year 1940 the human population doubled, then from 1940 to '98 it doubled again; and it will double again by 2056. And guess what? Then we really won't have to worry about recycling bottles because civilization will have expired. Somebody will have killed the last deer, caught the last fish, and chopped up the last piece of firewood. But when you talk about those things, you're suddenly into religion, ethnicity, contraception, and all those things that people loathe to discuss. So it's a sad thing to watch.

You read about all these wonderful people saying they're going to do something. Well, do something where it hurts. Do something where it's real. This is it.

Of course, anyone can probably take my remarks and say, "Well, if that isn't high drama; that's Simpson." I wish there were a more adroit and Shakespearean way to say it. Shakespeare used some powerful words. I try not to use the word *bullshit* too much, but it's such a marvelous word, and strictly out of the lexicon of

Wyoming. It does cut through the crap, and that's where we are now. And what are we doing about real things? Nothing!

As to population, education of women is a key. When women are educated, the fertility rate goes down dramatically. That is the issue. There is no bigger issue than that.   *April 23, 1998*

Visualize a perfect world? This is appalling for me! I've never used any kind of paint. What the hell am I doing here? Unbelievable! Bizarre!

I recall:

When Earth's last picture is painted and the tubes are twisted and dried,
When the oldest colors have faded, and the youngest critic has died,
We shall rest, and, faith, we shall need it—lie down for an aeon or two,
Till the Master of All Good Workmen shall put us to work anew!

And those that were good shall be happy: they shall sit in a golden chair;
They shall splash at a ten-league canvas with brushes of comet's hair; . . .

And only the Master shall praise us, and only the Master shall blame;
And no one shall work for money, and no one shall work for fame,
But each for the joy of the working, and each, in his separate star,
Shall draw the Thing as he sees It for the God of Things as They Are!

Rudyard Kipling wrote that. Hard to believe. Sounds like someone else.

There's the high country. Then, you get down here in the timberline, and the grandeur of the lower basin near the Tetons. Bobcat Ranch there, punctuated by the little brown fences. We're not going to put any black cypress in here. But, of course, we do need a pine and a Douglas fir. A little footpath here. We should have a little Indian paintbrush. That's the state flower. Put that in the foreground. And here's one of the most unique plants the world has ever known, known only in the imagination. It doesn't have to be attached to the earth in any way; it's just floating. This is the damnedest interview I've ever had.

155

Daniel STEIN

Executive Director, Federation for American Immigration Reform (since 1988)

Daniel Stein has served as executive director of the Federation for American Immigration Reform (FAIR) since 1988. He is an expert on immigration policy and law, and a vocal advocate for immigration reform. Before joining FAIR, Stein was CEO of the public-interest Immigration Reform Law Institute. In that capacity he argued a number of important cases in federal district court and drafted several important briefs related to the balance of federalism in state-federal relations.

156

My perfect environment would be one in which I feel a strong sense of privacy and have room to wander, free of impediments. My sense of space and horizon would be constantly changing, which is consistent with my love of improvisation and jazz. The lack of predictability is important.

I could wander around, catlike, feeling the freedom to enjoy the natural wonders of a diversified topography with great climatic variations. I want control over my individual destiny, and I also want my environment to be not so densely populated that I'm constantly bumping into other humans.

I have a lot of favorite places, but the one thing they all have in common is that they're not full of people. The population/immigration issue is essentially a battle between those who think that population can grow, and that consumption patterns simply need to change, and those of us who believe that if population densities were low enough, individual liberty could be maintained without any great environmental degradation. That's where I am.

The most important thing about my perfect world, though, is that the human race will have adopted by clear consensus the overriding goal of small families. The livability of the planet is entirely dependent upon that. I do not want a world that's as populated as it is now, much less what it's going to be soon. So that's critical.

This is a picture of an environment where individuals have to take responsibility for the consequences of their actions. The only way to get that is through certain kinds of divisions. I constantly see people trying to get around the consequences of their own decisions, or whole societies trying to do that.

What I'm trying to show is a world of accountability, which means that these guys over here can't just spill over onto our space. We need the capacity to somehow shield ourselves, to define ourselves in a different area. One side is overpopulation, and the other side represents the kind of world I want to leave to my kids. Of course, as long as population is growing over here, our area's under threat, too.

157

There are still many countries, like the Philippines and Mexico, that maintain higher than replacement fertility rates because they have the expectation that kids will leave and send money back home. So immigration forestalls the necessary transition to more stable numbers. My most important hope is for a broad understanding of the fact that as population grows, individual liberties decline necessarily. We might be able to squeeze ten billion people into the United States, but at what cost to individual freedom? What kind of lives would we be living?

You know, environmentalism, as we inherited it from John Muir or Teddy Roosevelt, is an American cultural value that isn't necessarily shared by everybody. A lot of people are told that human beings were made to live like they do in Hong Kong, where the average person has eight square feet of space, and that if you don't agree with that, you're a nasty person.

I think people have to bloom where they're planted, and they have to take individual responsibility for their space. You can't junk other people's space because you're not responsible about your family-planning decisions. It's a radically new way of looking at things. For most of human history, if you fouled your own nest, you could just move on. But there are no more wilderness areas left to be populated.

Winston Churchill once said that a great way to find fascinating reading material is to take any book off the shelf, open up to any page, and just start reading. I don't feel the need to excessively plan, because I think in general good things happen. If you work hard, and try to make them happen, they will. I think people are inherently intelligent and rational and also remarkably flexible and adaptable, so if they feel there is a true and honest need to change their behavior, they will.

I am worried, though, about historically powerful institutions like the Roman Catholic Church, which has perpetuated itself through custom and habit, and which works hard to prevent people from thinking things through in rational ways. I'm also worried that this consumption-at-all-costs society is built on trying to get people to mass-produce and consume junk. And I just think we're losing our ability to imagine a higher-order world. You don't see a lot of visionary thinking in society today. I guess we spend so much time struggling with social crises, and worldwide frictions and migration flare-ups, that nobody's envisioning the utopian societies for the world.

April 18, 1997

Lester THUROW

Jerome and Dorothy Lemelson Professor of Management and Economics, Sloan School of Management, MIT

Lester Thurow has been a professor of management and economics at MIT for more than thirty years, beginning in 1968. He served as dean of the Sloan School from 1987 to 1993 and was coordinator of the MIT Asia-Pacific Initiatives. During the 1980s he was an editorial board member and columnist for *The New York Times*, a contributing editor for *Newsweek*, and a member of *Time* magazine's Board of Economics. He is the author of many books, including *The Zero Sum Game* (1980), *The Sum Solution* (1985), and *The Future of Capitalism* (1996).

I always say to my sons that having a job you like is heaven and having a job you dislike is hell because you've got to go, right? You've got to eat. But even if you're making a lot of money, and you hate your job, it's still a lousy job. Well, I like my job.

I'm a professor at MIT because I like this environment. I can act in individual ways that I couldn't dream of doing in any corporation. It allows me to be a big individual, with individual latitude, and also get institutional support, so that's very nice.

After I quit being dean here, I did six or seven outdoor adventures, and I liked that very much, too. I hunted polar bears with a camera in the Arctic. I did a safari through the desert called the Empty Quarter in southern Saudi Arabia. I went mountain climbing in the Himalayas. I went scuba diving in the Caribbean.

What's particularly great about Himalayan mountain climbing is that it's very clear to what degree you've succeeded or failed. That's the problem with being a professor—you write things and they kind of slide out there into the big world. Feedback is very murky at best. It's never really clear whether you make any difference. Nobody knows. But if you climb a Himalayan peak, you either get there or you don't. I am not a woman, obviously, but I think the only difference between writing a book and having a baby is that if you have a baby, the neighbors gather around and say, "It's a beautiful baby," even if it's ugly. They always say it's beautiful. But with a book, people get paid to say it's ugly, write ugly-baby reviews.

You mean there's supposed to be something visual about my ideal world? I haven't painted for a while. Actually, I know what I want to do. The question is how to do it. (People are usually only interested in what I think about economics.)

In my ideal world, everybody would have the chance to have some adventure. That doesn't necessarily mean going to the moon, but it does mean having a sense of excitement, discovering something new. It's like Jules Verne journeying to the center of the earth or the guys doing biotechnology. New frontiers. I'll take a rocket to the middle of the earth. Why not? I don't know exactly how to visualize intellectual adventures. Scientifically there are always new things to discover. We never reach the end. So here's a guy in his laboratory. We'll put test tubes on the table, even though people don't use test tubes anymore. I'm cheating here; I'm going to put in a formula—$e = mc^2$. And someone skywriting out the back end of an airplane. We'll put a little oil in the ground and have people searching for it. The oil industry at the moment is full of excitement because they've discovered the biggest oil fields in the world around the Caspian Sea. It's the modern equivalent of the Conquistadors who went to the New World looking for gold. Adventure.

I always say that when you no longer ask the question, What am I going to do when I grow up? the time has come to quit. I hope I'll still be asking that question when I'm eighty.

160

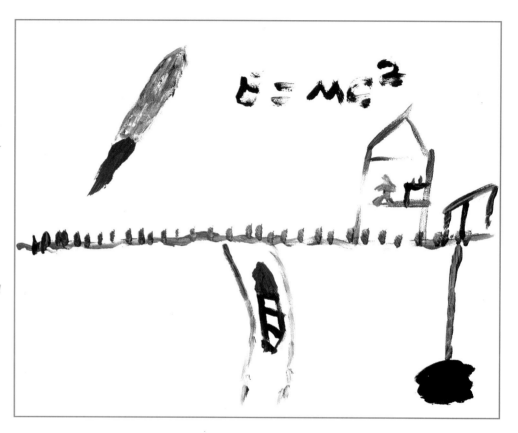

I think it would be very nice if we lived in the old-fashioned United States, which we haven't had for a quarter of a century, where if our economy goes up, everybody participates. Right now if the American economy goes up, 20 percent of us participate, 20 percent of us do okay, and 60 percent of us are in trouble. That's no good. You always want to live in a neighborhood where your neighbors are wealthier than you are, even if it makes you envious. It's much better than being a wealthy person in a poor neighborhood, which is the kind of society we're creating now.

Europeans look at our rapidly growing inequality and say, "Why isn't there any social protest?" The paper recently reported that Bill Gates has more wealth than the bottom 40 percent of all Americans—a hundred million people. But that news didn't seem to bother anybody in the United States. In 1996, when the French proposed to lay off twenty thousand people and cut pensions by a small amount, the whole country went up in smoke—burning tires, tractors blockading the road. Paris came to a halt for four weeks. At exactly the same time AT&T—one company—laid off fifty thousand people, more than the French were proposing to touch, and there wasn't a peep about it here.

In America if I get rich I get to say, "I got rich because Lester Thurow was smart." So if I become poor, I've got to say it was because Lester Thurow was dumb, right? But Europeans see being rich and poor as having a big social component. In the United States, homeless people on the street deserve to be homeless:

They're lazy, they're uneducated, whatever. We don't say something's wrong with the social system. It's just different.

I suppose the other thing one could hope for is a society that pays attention to the long term more than we do. There's a set of long-term things like environmentalism, investments in education, infrastructure, all the things that will make the world a better place ten or thirty years from now, that we Americans systematically underinvest in today.

The peculiar thing about the American education system is that it's the best in the world for the top 20 percent, but the worst in the entire industrial world for the bottom 20 percent. For them, it doesn't perform at all. We've got 25 percent of American young people dropping out of high school, which isn't true of any other industrial country.

Now, the problem is that since it's so good at the top, the people at the top don't want to change the system. They're afraid any change will make things worse for them, right? And the other thing is that this problem isn't solvable with money. You've got to do some major restructuring, and that means taking on entrenched American beliefs, like the belief that local school boards ought to run schools. We've got eight thousand school boards running schools in America, and this idea that parents care is just plain wrong. I mean, how can anybody run a high-quality school, flunk their neighbor's kid, and still get elected to the school board? Local school boards will never set high standards. They're elected because they set low standards so that everybody passes. That's how it works, and it's the biggest social problem in America. The sad thing about it is that we've been talking about this since at least 1981, and we haven't done anything. It's hard to know what to do.

May 13, 1998

Neil DE GRASSE TYSON

Frederick P. Rose Director, Hayden Planetarium, American Museum of Natural History (since 1996); Visiting Research Scientist, Department of Astrophysics, Princeton University (since 1994)

Neil de Grasse Tyson is the first Frederick P. Rose Director of the Hayden Planetarium at the American Museum of Natural History in New York City and a visiting research scientist in astrophysics at Princeton University, where he teaches. He writes a monthly column called "Universe" for *Natural History* magazine and is the author of several books, including *One Universe: At Home in the Cosmos* (2000) and *The Sky Is Not the Limit: Adventures of an Urban Astrophysicist* (2000).

My reading of history tells me that as often as people wish and pray for peace, a world without war just never works out. So, I think that's naive, and I don't hope without having an anchor in what's plausible. Otherwise I'd spend my life being disappointed.

What I hope for plausibly is the continuing realization of the Copernican principle, which asserts in its simplest form that we are not special in this universe. No matter how special you think you are, you are not. Now, that's kind of the antithesis of what goes on in psychological therapy sessions for people who need to improve their self-esteem. But it can actually be quite uplifting, as well as humbling. When you realize that we're just little specks crawling around on a hunk of dirt, which is itself a speck in orbit around a single star that's just one among over a hundred billion stars in the galaxy, these are humbling facts.

It will be even more humbling when we find evidence of life elsewhere in the universe, at least a fossil record. We know that wherever there is liquid water and the right ingredients, the natural course of evolution leads compellingly to life. So when we discover that life once existed on Mars or on Europa, say, that will humble us further. And I think that's an important posture to take. I call it the cosmic perspective.

You see people waging war, and ask, "Why?" When an astronomer asks that question, it's because in the context of the universe there's a limit to how much you can believe you're more important

I have a simple image in my head. I was born and raised in New York City, so I'm a city person. But the universe calls. My first time in the Hayden Planetarium I was nine years old, and along the periphery was the Manhattan skyline and Central Park in front. It was the most beautiful thing I'd ever seen. I will not stand in denial of civilization, or technology, but I will also not deny myself the simple pleasure of looking up. That's what binds us to all other humans. To me there's something peaceful about this image. It's the juxtaposition of nature, civilization, and the universe. It's my life!

than someone else. So in that regard astronomers are the most utopian people around, because we're not burdened by any great concern about politics or national boundaries.

We also bring answers to the questions that have prevailed for centuries and across cultures, like What is our place in the universe? Where is it going? and Where did it all come from? We're starting to answer those questions now, so it's a happy time to be alive. We don't need to resort to mythology.

What I want to promote more than anything else in the world is rational thought, as opposed to irrational thought, which I think there is far too much of. For instance, there are always people who know about probabilities, who will take advantage of people who don't. It's hard to be a functioning member of society and not understand how probabilities work. The lottery is not a tax on the poor; it's a tax on people who don't do well in mathematics. I want to promote a world where people are trained in how to think rationally about how the world works. Knowing facts about science is important, but knowing how to think matters more.

If people were trained in how to think, we would live in a much stronger society, a society less prone to superstition. We're supposed to be masters of our own destiny. We're not supposed to be just victims; we're not just slaves to the forces around us. But if we abandon our intellectual powers, I would say we're an embarrassment to our species, and we might as well slither back down into the mud and join the rest of the worms.

Raising my children is the most rewarding and fulfilling thing I've ever done. I get no end of pleasure in watching their minds develop. Every weekend we try to do at least one science experiment in the kitchen, so that they begin to see how the world works and start finding patterns. Watching the young mind develop is a privilege and an honor, and it's the thing I want to do more than anything else.

I also give students much more attention than I give adults, because you've got to keep the wheel turning. When I was a student, I met with Carl Sagan in his office at Cornell and he spent time with me. He didn't know me from anybody; I was just a senior in high school. But I told myself then that if I were ever in a position of influence, I would model my encounter with students after how I was treated by Carl Sagan. And I have.

I regret that, in my capacity as director, I now do much less night observing than I once did. There's something emotionally fulfilling and even spiritual about your encounter with light at the top of a mountain. But I'm in a different chapter in my life now, where more of my effort is invested in helping others, and I certainly don't regret that.

At some point I realized that I was no longer just a scientist; I was a servant of society. That was a profound realization. It means I have a talent set and a pedigree that allows me to enrich other people's lives, so I can no longer be selfish. I can no longer say I just want to do my own work.

I love living every month into the future, and I salivate over new discoveries we make about the world around us. There's no time in the past that I would rather have been alive. I see pictures made in the 1880s and say, "That's quaint." But you had to worry about polio. There were no refrigerators. Plus, if I lived in those times, I'd be shining someone's shoes instead of being an astrophysicist. A hundred years before that, I'd have been a slave. There is no time in the past that I'd rather be living.

July 23, 2001

Sanford UNGAR

President, Goucher College (since 2001);
Director, Voice of America (1998–2000)

Sanford Ungar became president of Goucher College in July 2001 after having served as director of Voice of America (VOA), the U.S. government's principal international broadcasting agency, for two years. Before that he had been dean of the School of Communications at American University, host of NPR's *All Things Considered*, Washington editor of *The Atlantic Monthly*, and managing editor of *Foreign Policy*.

I idealize small-town life in America. In fact, I'm obsessed with it. When I think about this fantasy, I'm in a small town where I know a lot of people and can trust the way they present themselves to me. And the way you present yourself to them is imbued with good faith. This must sound terribly naive, but I have some very fond memories of growing up, even though I had a very difficult childhood, actually.

My father died when I was very young and was sick for quite a few years before that. Actually, there were a lot of family members dying during my childhood, I mean a lot. But I found people very supportive of one another, very meaningfully there for each other: neighbors, friends, relatives. And this is even though my mother's family would have these great, flat-out feuds, kind of like a Barry Levinson movie. And then everybody would make up at the funerals. As absurd and outrageous as it was, intense sometimes, there was something reassuring about it, too. It seemed like a more manageable world.

Another important thing about my ideal is that people around the world will understand each other better. I lived in Paris for a year and a half, a very formative time for me as a young journalist working for UPI. I speak French, and love being in France, despite all the infuriating things about the French people.

I've been in enough places around the world where the people are victims of their circumstance,

167

not just politically but economically, or with sicknesses, or climate—vulnerable to everything, and unable to do anything about it. I really do think that when other people are hungry, we are hungry. I think this country is much too selfish and self-centered, and I think it's getting worse. The decline in our awareness of the world is quite worrisome.

If I were thinking about the whole world, really, basic literacy would be a top priority. I think literacy means more than just being able to read. It means literacy about your own life and the world around you, being able to understand why different things matter more than you might have thought at first. So that's part of it.

I also worry about values in this country. I mean, I worry about this culture of acquisition and materialism. I'm bothered by the way people use material things like cars to present themselves to the world. I have such a visceral negative reaction to a Mercedes that I almost couldn't ride in one. I just think Mercedes are symbols of what's wrong with our consumer culture, not to mention that they were a Nazi company that was never fully de-Nazified.

I'm very involved with my children, and I really worry about the world they have to live in. It's a selfish, nasty, harsh world, the kind of place where you always have to look out to make sure you're not being cheated or tricked. Both of my kids are very generous people, and sometimes I think I've done them a terrible disservice, because they've got a squishy-soft, foggy-headed father in some ways.

April 28, 1997

I feel like I'm being interviewed for nursery school, and how well I draw and play will determine whether I get in. My nervous parents are watching me through the one-way glass. You know, I think painting is something we have the ability to do at some stage in our life, and then lose. This is a very unusual thing for you to ask.

Actually, it's an interesting challenge. How would I picture some of what I've been describing? First, there would be children in my perfect world, but I'm not good at drawing children. I associate orange with happiness. I don't know why. The triangles are deltas for change—positive change, because they're in an optimistic color. And this is a rising sun. So there you have it. I don't think I'd get into a very good nursery school with this painting.

I wanted to use a lot of positive colors to show a lot of good things happening. This painting represents an alternative to a kind of dull sameness and uniformity, every place looking the same as every place else, having the same shopping malls, and Flash! Interest! Excitement!

J. Craig VENTER

President and Chief Scientific Officer, Celera Genomics Corporation (1998–2002); Founder, Chairman, and Chief Scientist, Institute for Genomic Research (since 1992)

170

J. Craig Venter is the founder of Celera Genomics Corporation, the world's largest laboratory for unraveling the precise order of any genome, and for four years served as its president and chief scientific officer. In June 2000 Venter and the director of the publicly funded Human Genome Project stood together in a White House ceremony marking their historic success at mapping the complete human genome. Venter is also the founder and chairman of the Institute for Genomic Research (TIGR), a not-for-profit genomics research institute.

I generally create the kind of environment that I thrive in, and the components of that are right here at Celera. We're dealing with one of the biggest, if not *the* biggest, science projects in the world. Right now we're working to sequence the drosophila genome, the human genome, the mouse genome, and the rice genome. I'm surrounded by highly intelligent, highly motivated people, so there's never a dull day. And there's a higher purpose to what we're doing, lots of them actually. The nutshell one is that we're trying to change society, change the future of humanity. So we have modest goals. . . .

I hope for a world where disease is far less prevalent in people's lives. And I also hope for a whole lot better control over population. We have to get there fairly soon. I'm actually more concerned about that than I am with curing disease. Some people claim that curing disease will contribute to increasing the population. But, of course, the answer is not to let people die early deaths from disease, or starve to death, as a means of controlling the population. History has shown that improving the health of the population actually goes hand in hand with a decrease, not an increase, in birth rate.

The goal is not to prolong life but to change the quality of life during a normal life period. In the 1990s, five million people died from cancer in the United States, and obviously a lot of those were young people. That's just one disease that has had a devastating impact. What we really want to

Oh oh. I'm definitely not a visual thinker. I have no visual memory whatsoever. If I close my eyes, I see no pictures at all.

This painting is about the continued evolution of life, knowledge, hopefully of the planet, not necessarily by changing. . . . I indeed do hope humans will change, but not by manufactured means necessarily. The brown is the earthy base. Yellow is enlightenment. (Good enlightenment color.) I don't think this painting will sell for much. Definitely not van Gogh's wheat fields. This was a hard assignment.

do is empower individuals, give people information about their own genetic makeup that will give them power for the first time to understand their futures.

A few years ago we discovered genes that cause colon cancer. So by understanding the spelling changes in those genes, we can determine who has a very increased likelihood of getting colon cancer. That would be nice for them to know, because the treatment for colon cancer is highly effective *if* it's caught early. If it's not, the effects are usually devastating, after a huge expense. If you knew you had a greatly increased chance of getting this cancer, you could get regular prediagnostic checks and find it early. And that's just one of probably twenty or thirty thousand examples of how this information we're finding can be used.

We're going to soon have the complete genetic code of humans, and that means we'll be starting from a new point of knowledge. At the start of this decade there were less than two thousand of the eighty thousand human genes known. And yet if you went to your physician, he had this view that he knew virtually everything there was to know about human biology. In actual fact, we're still just coming out of the Dark Ages. I think genomics will be viewed historically as the turning point for that.

So, we're raising the knowledge level in the world, and that will have all kinds of implications, most of them good. It will turn biology and medicine upside down, because we'll have to explain all the biology, all the physiology, all the function, of an organism

using the genetic components that we know are there. What would the future be like without this genomic information is an important question to ask. It would be one of greatly increased fear and death from bacterial and parasitic disease.

I think the next few decades in science are going to be some of the most remarkable times we've ever had. Phenomenally exciting. We're laying the foundation; DNA is the foundation of the future. If I felt the negative aspects of this research were the principal outcome, we wouldn't do this work. But my biggest concern about all this on the negative side is bad science, and bad press—reporters who want to make sensational claims and scientists making marginal links that don't hold up.

One diabolical scenario I can think of is for someone to genotype all the people in prison for child molestation and find common changes in their genetic code. Then they could say, "Here's the genotype for a child molester." And then they might go out and test the population, and say, "Since you have the genotype for child molestation, maybe we should lock you up, in advance." I don't think that kind of scenario is out of the question, but that would definitely be a result of bad, sloppy science. You may have the genotype for a child molester (if there is such a thing), but it's still within your capacity to act on those urges or not. So, I think it will come down to fundamental questions about who we are as humans.

I don't rule out that someday we'll be trying to modify the human genetic code. At least I think a lot of people will consider doing that, if they consider doing it now. Right now, even if people think they can do it, it absolutely shouldn't be done, because we're not smart enough yet. We don't have enough fundamental knowledge to do it intelligently. Genes interact in vast networks. It's not as simple as if you took the spark plug out of an engine and all of a sudden the engine didn't work anymore.

But I don't think manipulating the human genome would necessarily be fundamentally wrong. It depends on what the changes are, and what the purpose is. I wouldn't mind having a little slot where I could plug a better memory chip into my brain, just as I can with my computer.

The same tools we're developing here are going to be key in helping to clean up the environment. We've done so much environmental damage that if we don't start becoming much more aware of it, there could be far more serious problems soon. It all links to the same things, overpopulation and overconsumption.

May 22, 1999

Jim WALLIS

Founder and Editor, Sojourners *magazine (since 1975); Activist, Author, and Commentator*

Jim Wallis is the founding editor of *Sojourners* magazine and a national commentator, activist, and speaker on ethics and public life. He convened Call to Renewal, a national federation of churches and faith-based organizations working to overcome poverty. He is the author of several books, including *Faith Works* (2000) and *Who Speaks for God?* (1996). *Time* magazine named Wallis among the Fifty Faces for America's Future.

I don't believe in utopias. I just know what religious people should be fighting for. We had the civil rights movement because Martin Luther King, Jr., insinuated religious values into the public conversation. And his vision, which is mine, too, is of a beloved community where all of us have a place at the table. I love the image of a table where there's room for everybody. Expand the table. Change the shape of the table. Make it a round table. That's the image, the vision, we're always fighting for. We fight for racial justice because it's a religious value. We fight for gender equality because it's a religious value. We fight for dignity and opportunity because those are religious values.

I'm probably most comfortable in a local community setting, where there are real people, often young people from the streets, trying to solve their violence problem. People ask me, "Aren't you scared?" and that never enters my mind. I like that environment better than I like speaking to congresspeople on Capitol Hill. I do both, you know.

Another environment I like is one where people are really hungry and searching for spiritual values. Where the spiritual questions are out on the table and no one's pushing them off. Politicians tend to dwell on issues of power, constituency, access. They're nervous about discussions of moral values, and even more worried about spirituality. Whenever that word comes up, someone mentions gurus and crystals. The worst thing is to speak about religious values as if they had some connection to politics. I believe in separation of church and state, but that doesn't mean you're supposed to keep

God out of public discourse. Religious values are critical in the public arena, and they're also very practical.

We just had a summit in Philadelphia, and I was one of the cochairs of the faith community part of it. You know, for two days you heard presidents and Colin Powell and corporate leaders say, "Our priority is our poorest, at-risk children; that's why we're here." Well, poor kids don't come first; they come last. The Hebrew prophets said that a nation's righteousness is determined by how it treats the poorest and most vulnerable. That's a religious value. You never get to that realization any other way, because poor welfare moms have the least amount of clout over policies. Ninety-three percent of all cuts made so far have been made to entitlements for the poor. The burden's felt by those who already have the most burden to bear. Now even if you don't like the welfare system, that's just absurdly unfair and unjust. It's religiously obscene.

The biggest contribution that religious people can make to the social process is hope. Not hope as a feeling or a mood, but hope as a commitment. Desmond Tutu used to say, "We are prisoners of hope in South Africa." In South Africa before the change, with Nelson Mandela in prison, the only spokespeople were church people like Desmond Tutu, and they were under tremendous pressure, death threats, et cetera. So I literally snuck into the country to support them for several weeks in 1988, which was a critical period.

Anyway, the first day I was there, Desmond Tutu rises to preach in St. George's Cathedral. (Our rally had been canceled by the police,

so we held a religious service instead; they couldn't cancel that.) The police in massive numbers are outside in riot gear, threatening and intimidating people. And on the inside the people are worshiping. Along the wall you have police tape-recording everything Desmond says. He's just this little man, but he's so confident, and he says: "This system of apartheid cannot endure, because it's evil." And then he points his finger at the police. "You are very powerful," he says. "But you are not gods. And I serve a God who cannot be mocked. In fact, you have already lost." And from behind the pulpit he flashes that big Desmond Tutu smile. And then he says, "Since you have already lost, why don't you come in and join the winning side?" I saw Bishop Tutu again later and asked him if he remembered that day. He said, "Yes, and that's what happened. They all joined our winning side." Hope is the single most powerful weapon we have for social change.

One hope I have is that we rescue a generation of children from annihilation. Our children in the cities, especially, are drowning in their own blood. They're killing one another and they're being killed by poverty. A few months ago I was driving home and drove straight into a machete fight—three kids chasing a fourth with machetes. They were going to kill him. This is in broad daylight, people out pushing strollers, and our children are chasing one another with machetes. I positioned my truck to block the attack; he jumped in the back, and I drove him away to safety. But he ran away, too scared even to let me take him to the hospital. So I mopped up all the blood from the back of my truck.

This drawing is of a table, a round table. And it's got people of all colors and shapes in a circle. You have gang leaders and CEOs. (I've literally been at a table with gang leaders and CEOs, both.) The problem is that these tables have become islands. The ocean is swirling around, and on the islands everyone feels alone, so the ocean becomes the focus. The islands are really great places to be, but how are we going to connect the islands? We need to expand them, and expand their influence so that more and more people can be touched, and so that teachings from the islands can create new social policies, new visions.

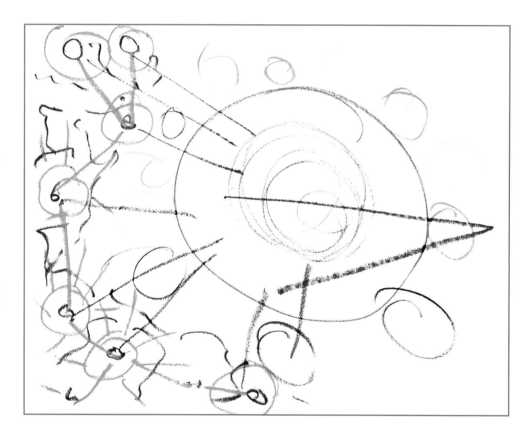

Now, when kids are chasing one another with knives and guns, we don't have a youth crisis, we have a societal crisis. And that's what we face now; we're losing a whole generation. So, I want to rescue that generation from this culture that's killing them.

Gandhi described the seven deadly sins as politics without principle, wealth without work, commerce without morality, education without character, pleasure without conscience, science without humanity, and worship without sacrifice. Those seven deadly sins have become our way of life. And when you have that kind of moral breakdown, the first ones to suffer are the young, the vulnerable, and those already on the edge.

Number two, I'd like to rescue the political system from the influence of money—campaign finance reform. Not just a few marginal laws but literally take money out of politics, so anybody can run on the basis of good ideas. Unless we do that, we're not going to make any progress on social issues.

Finally, I want our children to have life interactions every day that are broadly multicultural. I want white kids and black kids and Hispanic kids and Asian kids to just expect to live shoulder to shoulder, and expect that all their friendships will in fact reflect that very different vision. We're talking about people knowing from whence they came (no one wants to deny them who they are), but knowing also that who they are together is more important than who they are separately.

There's an image in my mind of "the islands of our work." I love that image. All the good things happening around the country, all the projects and grassroots efforts, are like little islands. And the raging ocean is between them. If you can swim to an island, you're going to be okay, but the islands need to be connected. They need to be expanded. Addiction, youth violence, job creation, housing, domestic abuse, teenage pregnancy, all that. We need a massive effort to map and network, and basically create, a new third-sector politics. The market and government still dominate everything in America, including volunteer efforts. We've got to elevate and strengthen the civil society—all the nonprofit organizations, all the churches and synagogues—to a status at least equal to the government and the market.

May 1, 1997